Mystical Owls Coloring Book

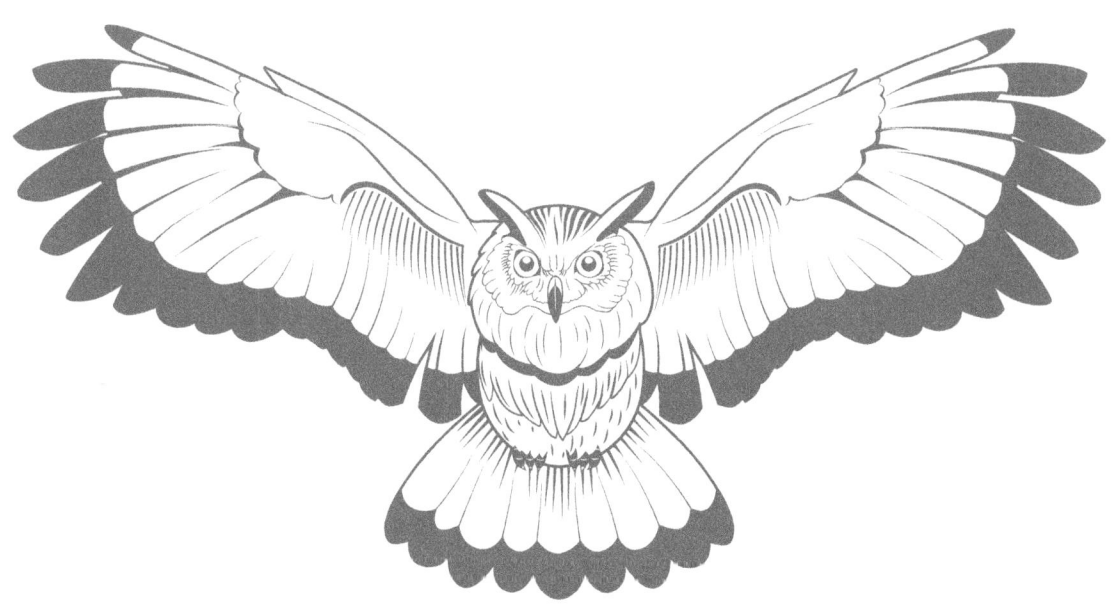

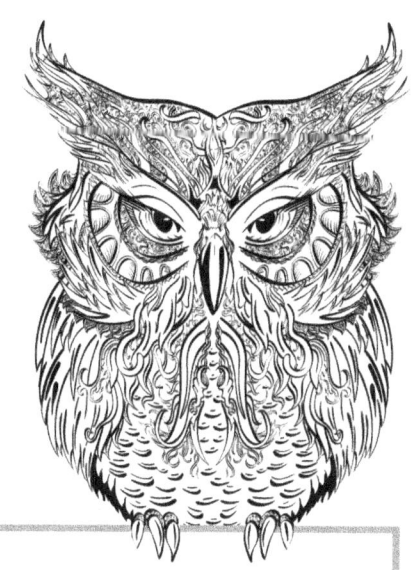

Mystical Owls Coloring Book
Color Yourslef Calm with Bea*hoo*tiful Illustrations

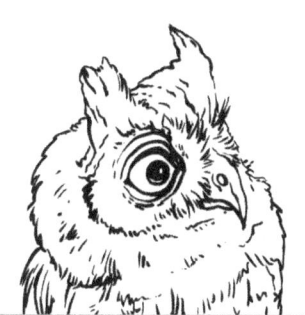 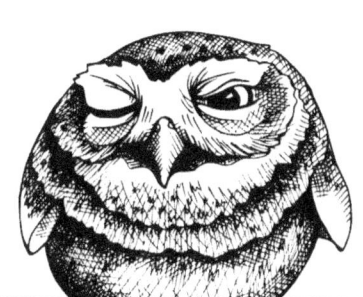 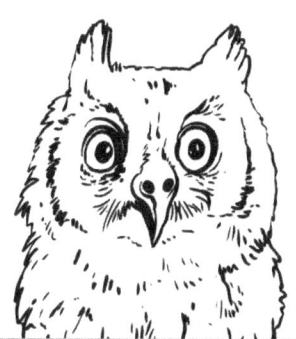

Image Credits:
Unless otherwise noted, all images are sourced from shutterstock.com
Cover Image © karakotsya; Back Cover Images © zhekakopylov, © Afishka, © Jakphoomin Phonnok, © panki; Page 1 © Alexander_P; Page 3 © zhekakopylov, © Afishka; Page 5 © tets; Page 7 © diana pryadieva; Page 9 © Mrs. Opossum; Page 11 © Suchkova Anna; Page 13 © Hein Nouwens; Page 15 © zhekakopylov; Page 17 © panki; Page 19 © Kateika; Page 21 © blackstroke; Page 23 © Jakphoomin Phonnok; Page 25 © wild0wild; Page 27 © Afishka; Page 29 © karakotsya; Page 31 © greenga; Page 33 © Jakphoomin Phonnok; Page 35 © Afishka; Page 37 © Imagepluss; Page 39 © DiviVector; Page 41 © ALEXEY GRIGOREV; Page 43 © zhekakopylov; Page 45 © Afishka; Page 47 © lurii Augulis; Page 49 © Yusyka; Page 51 © ARTdeeva; Page 53 © zhekakopylov; Page 55 © Kateika; Page 57 © SVR Studio; Page 59 © Imagepluss; Page 61 © Kateika; Page 63 © Kateika; Page 65 © Mehendra_art; Page 67 © karakotsya; Page 69 © Hein Nouwens; Page 71 © karakotsya; Page 73 © zhekakopylov; Page 75 © Julia Waller; Page 77 © Afishka; Page 79 © Alexander_P

Printed by: Createspace.com

10 9 8 7 6 5 4 3 2 1

June 2015
New York, New York, USA

More Books In This Collection:

Enchanted Birds Coloring Journal: A Six-Month Coloring Book and Journal to Calm the Mind and Record Your Thoughts

Calming Mandala Activity Book: Zen Drawings to Design, Doodle and Color for Mindfulness and Relaxation

Pocket Mandalas Coloring Book: Mini Zen Creations for Portable Relaxation and Mindfulness

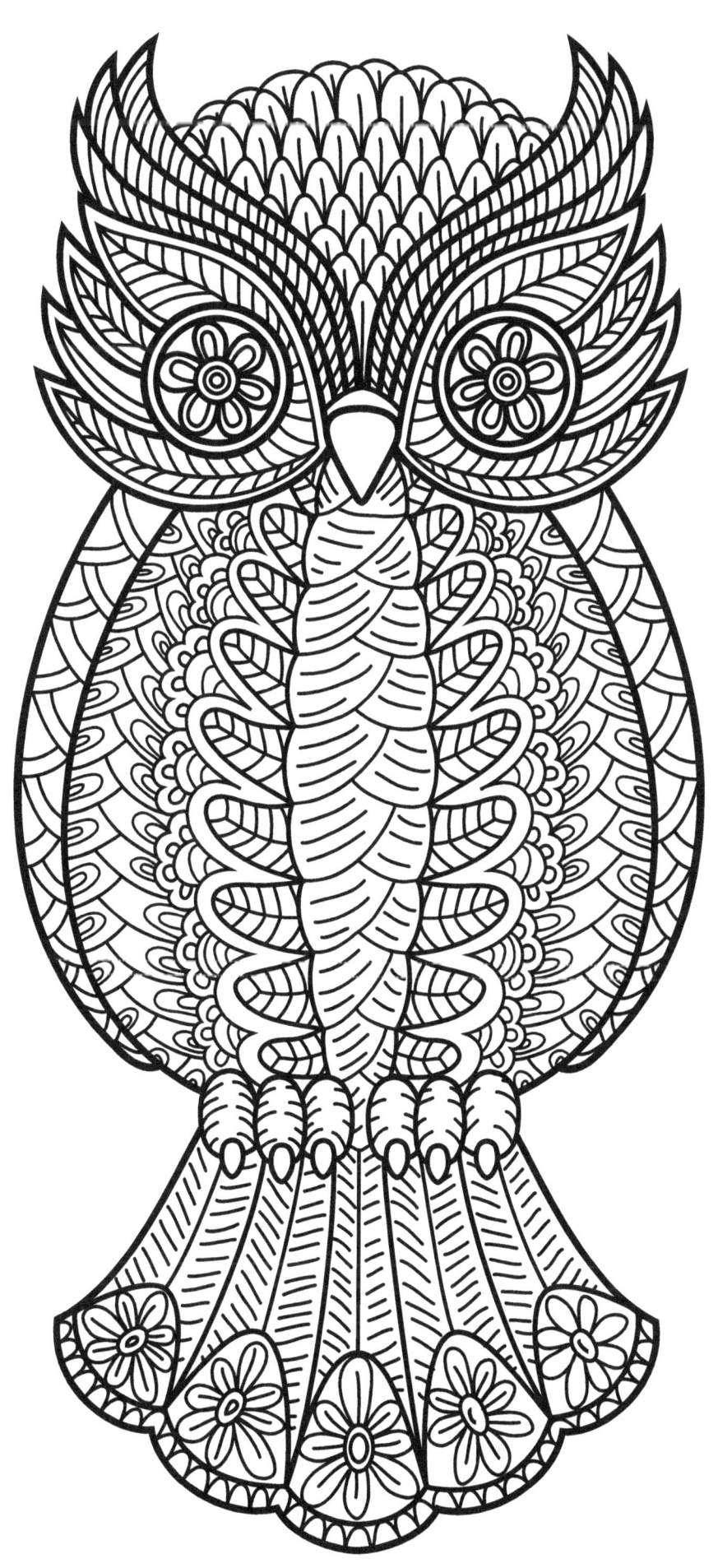

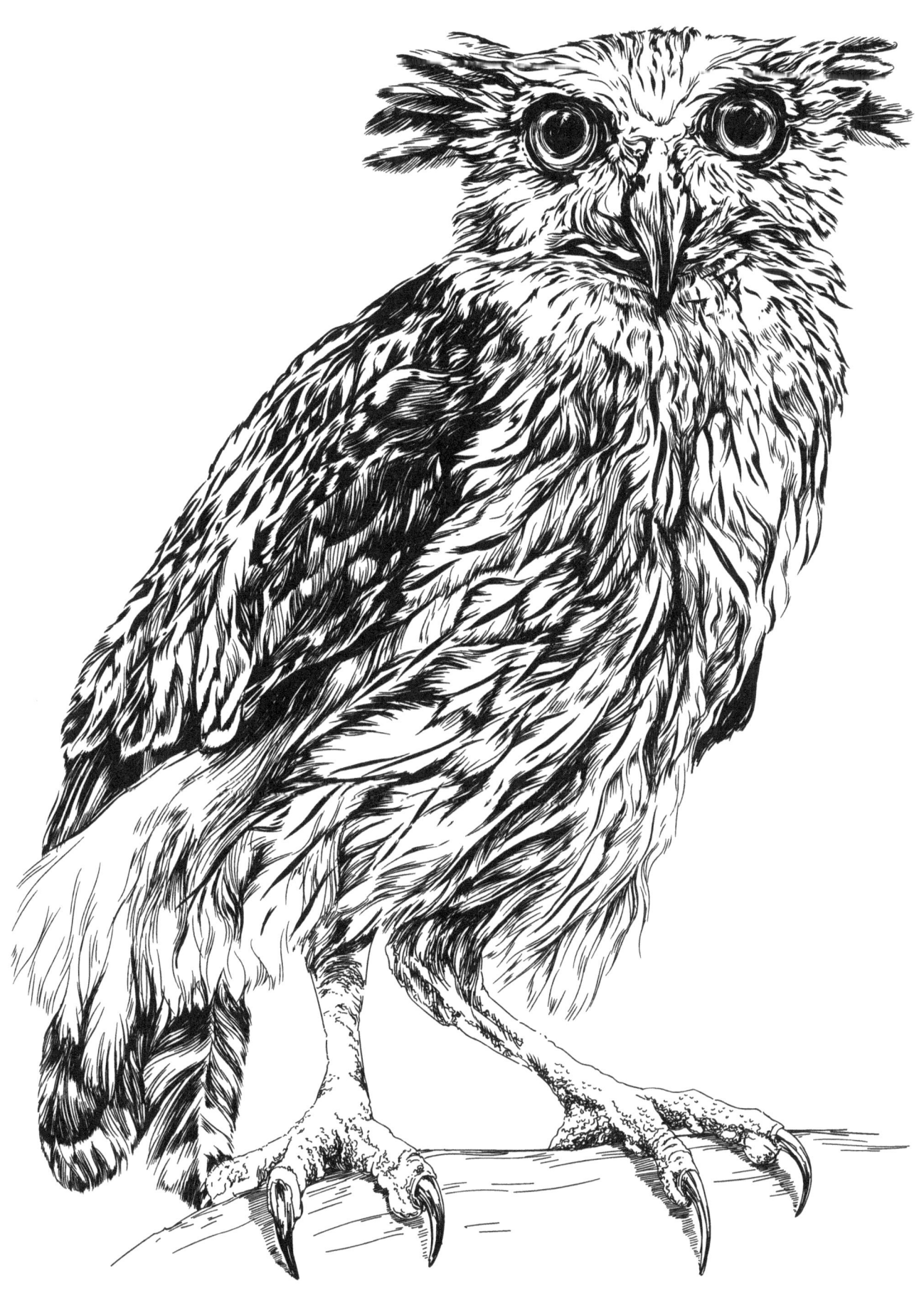

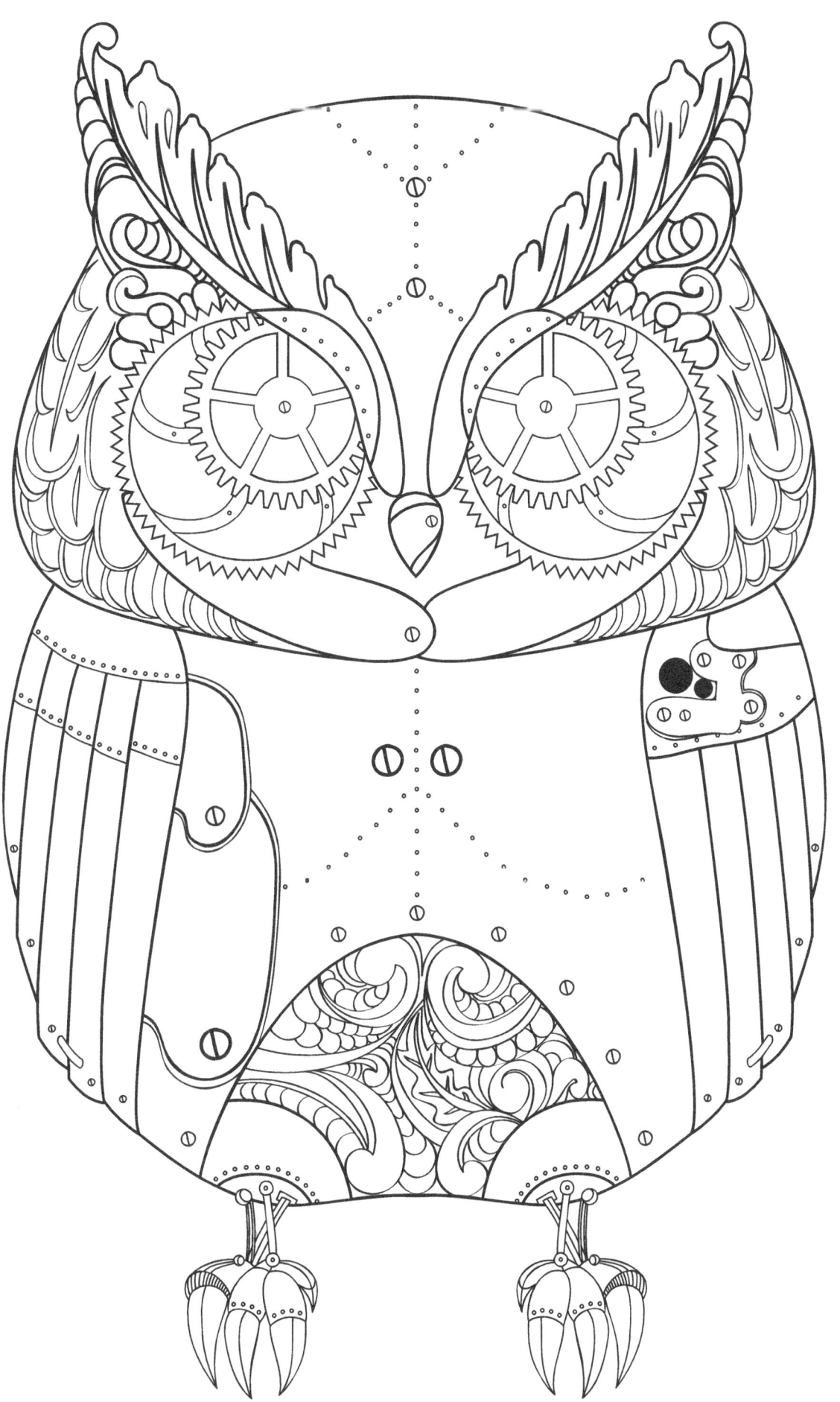

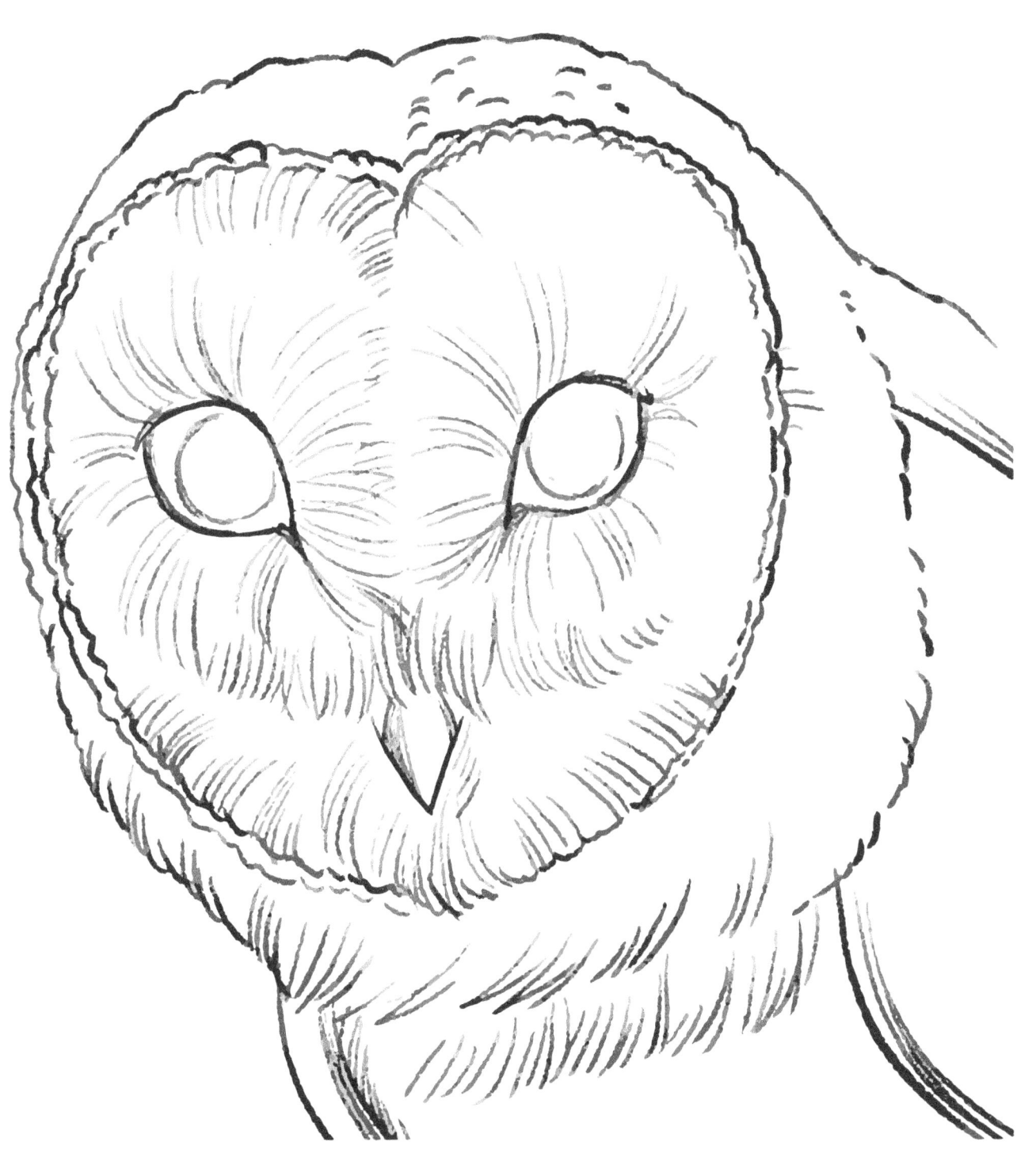

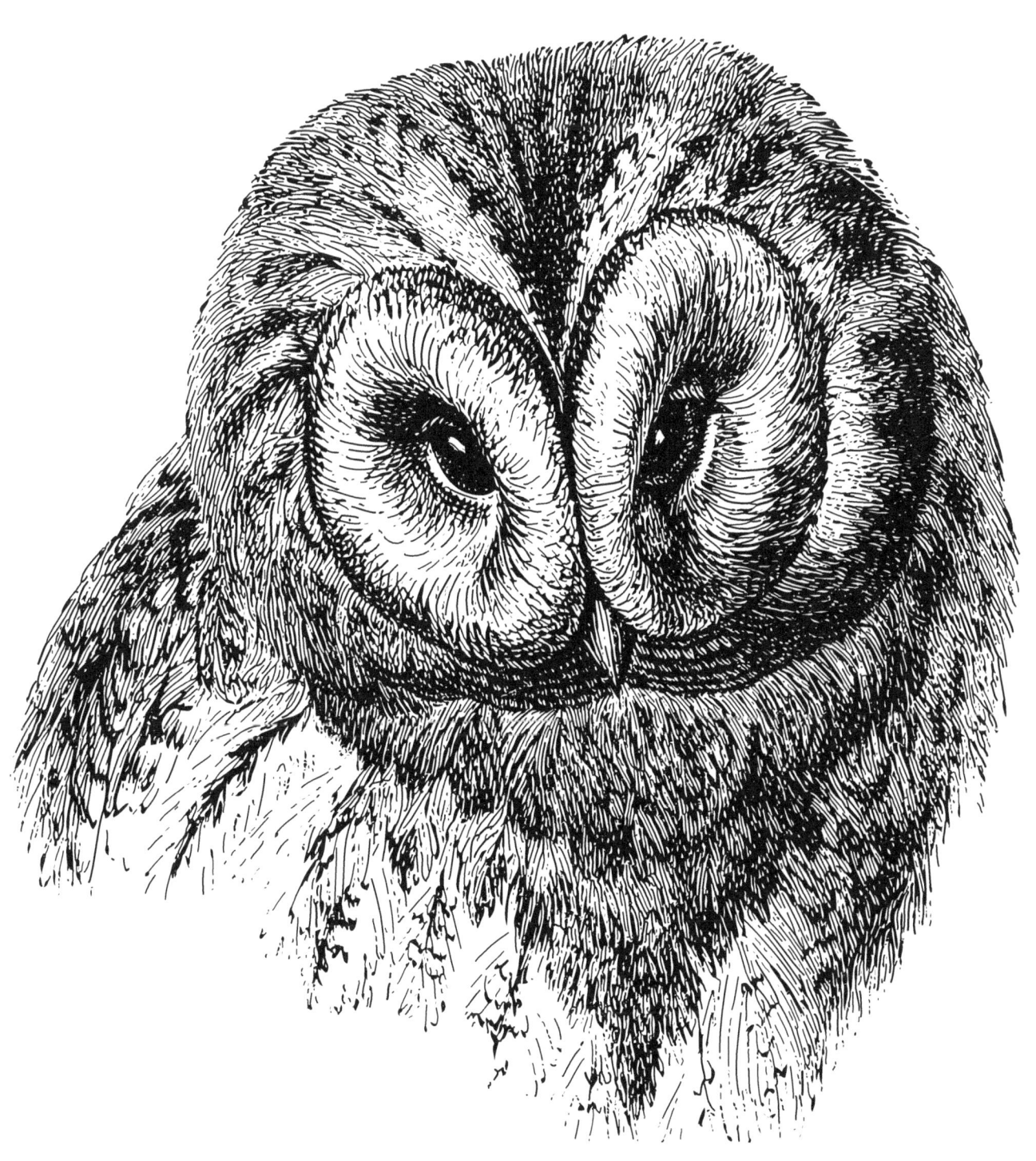

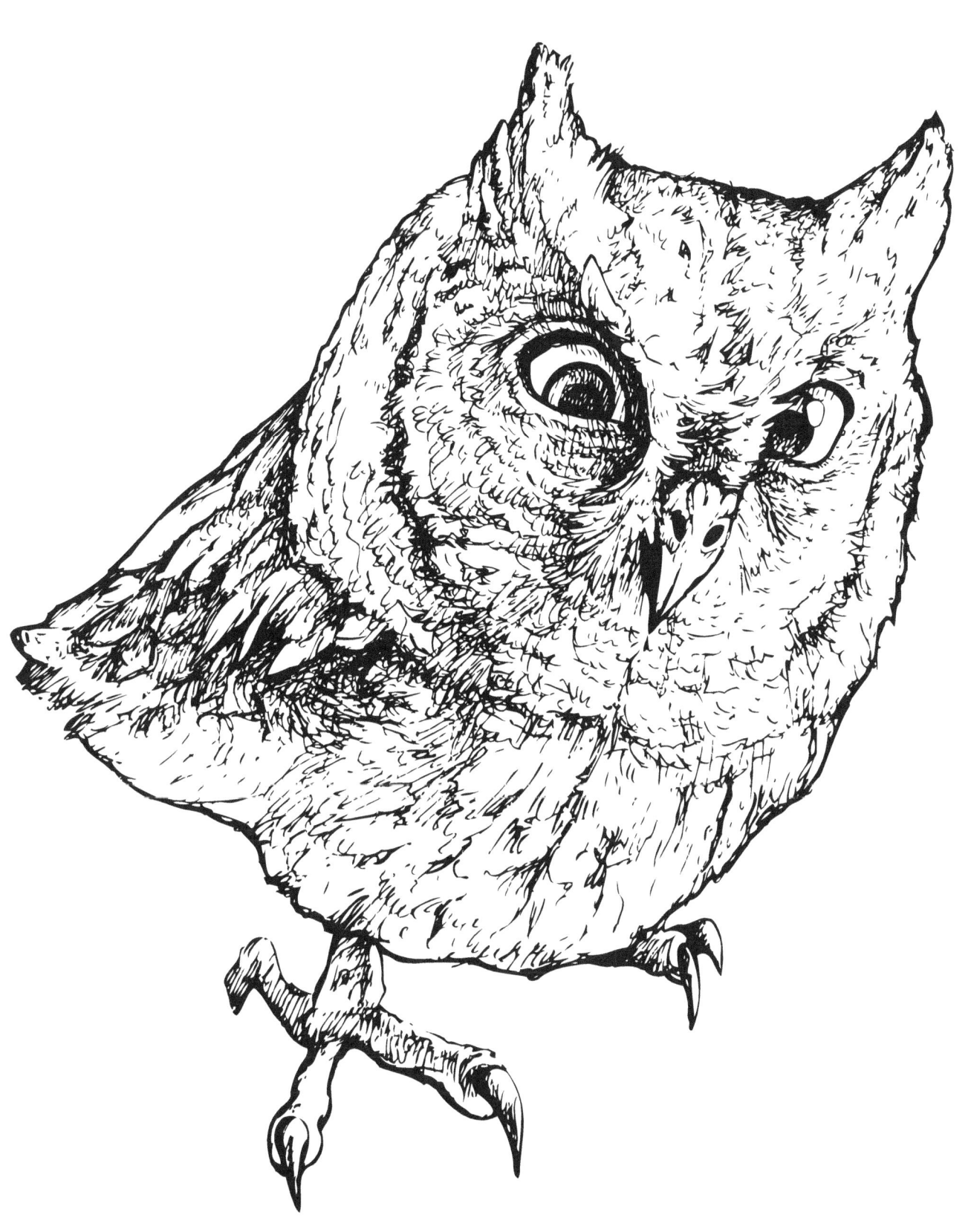

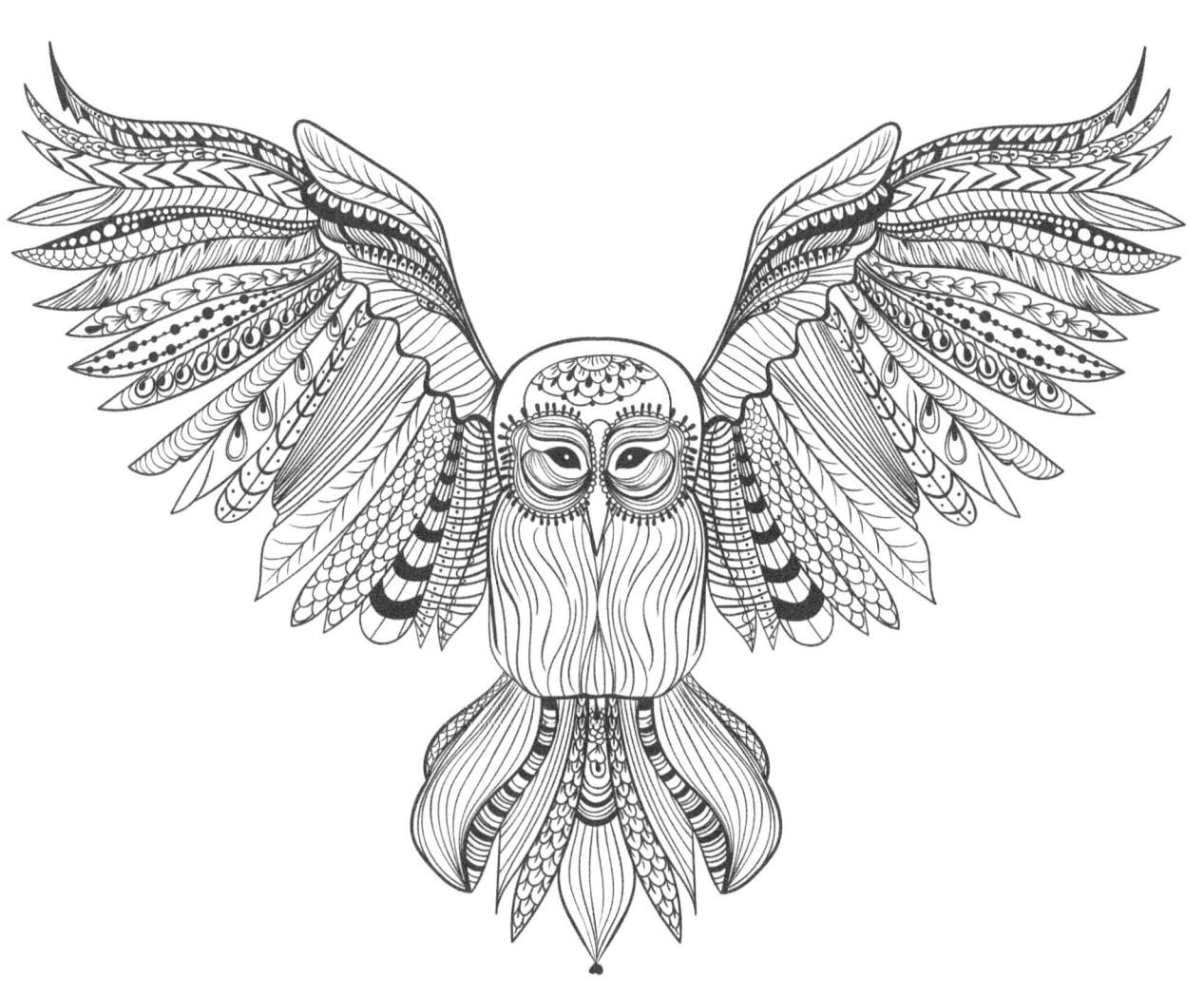

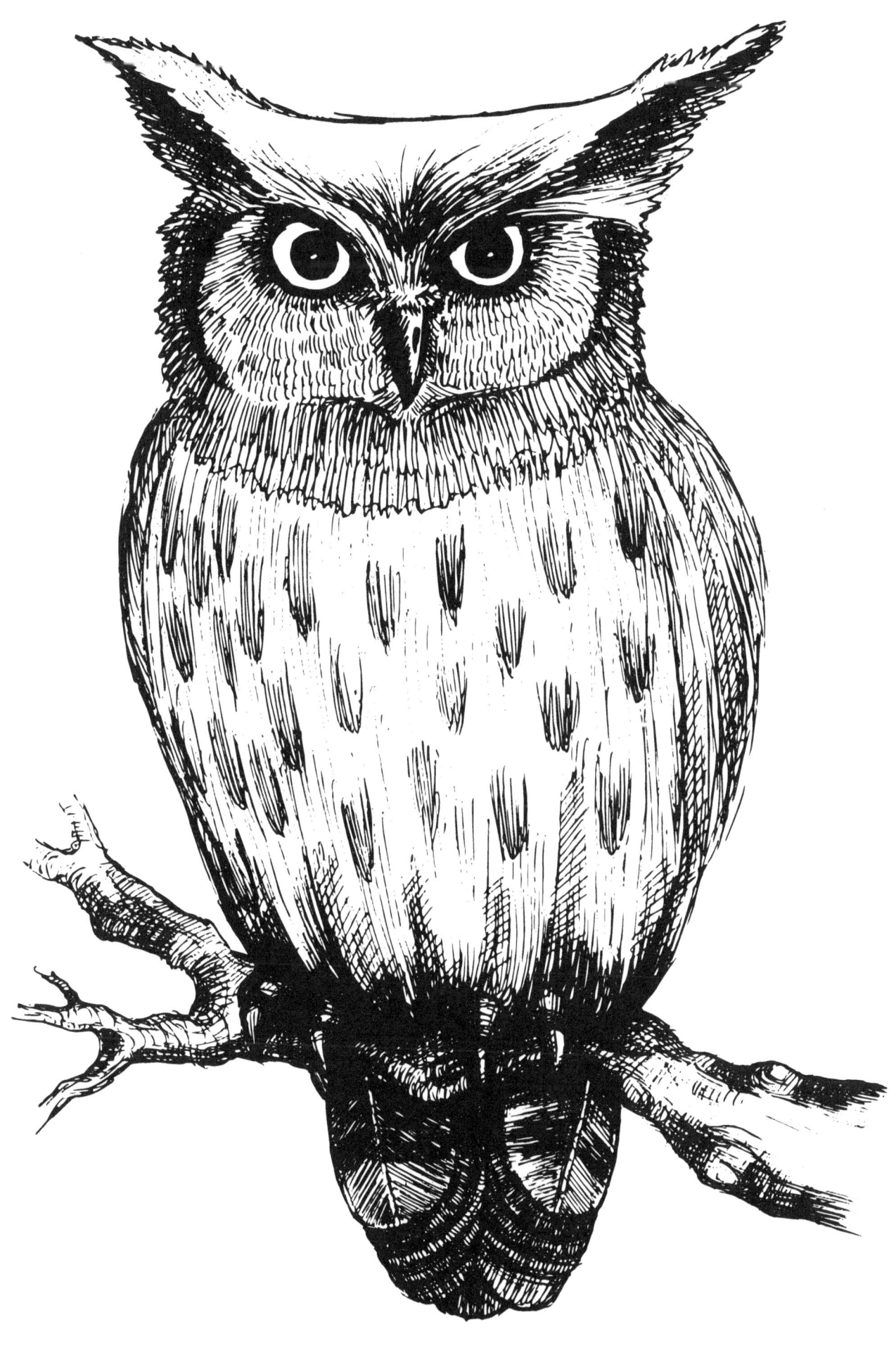

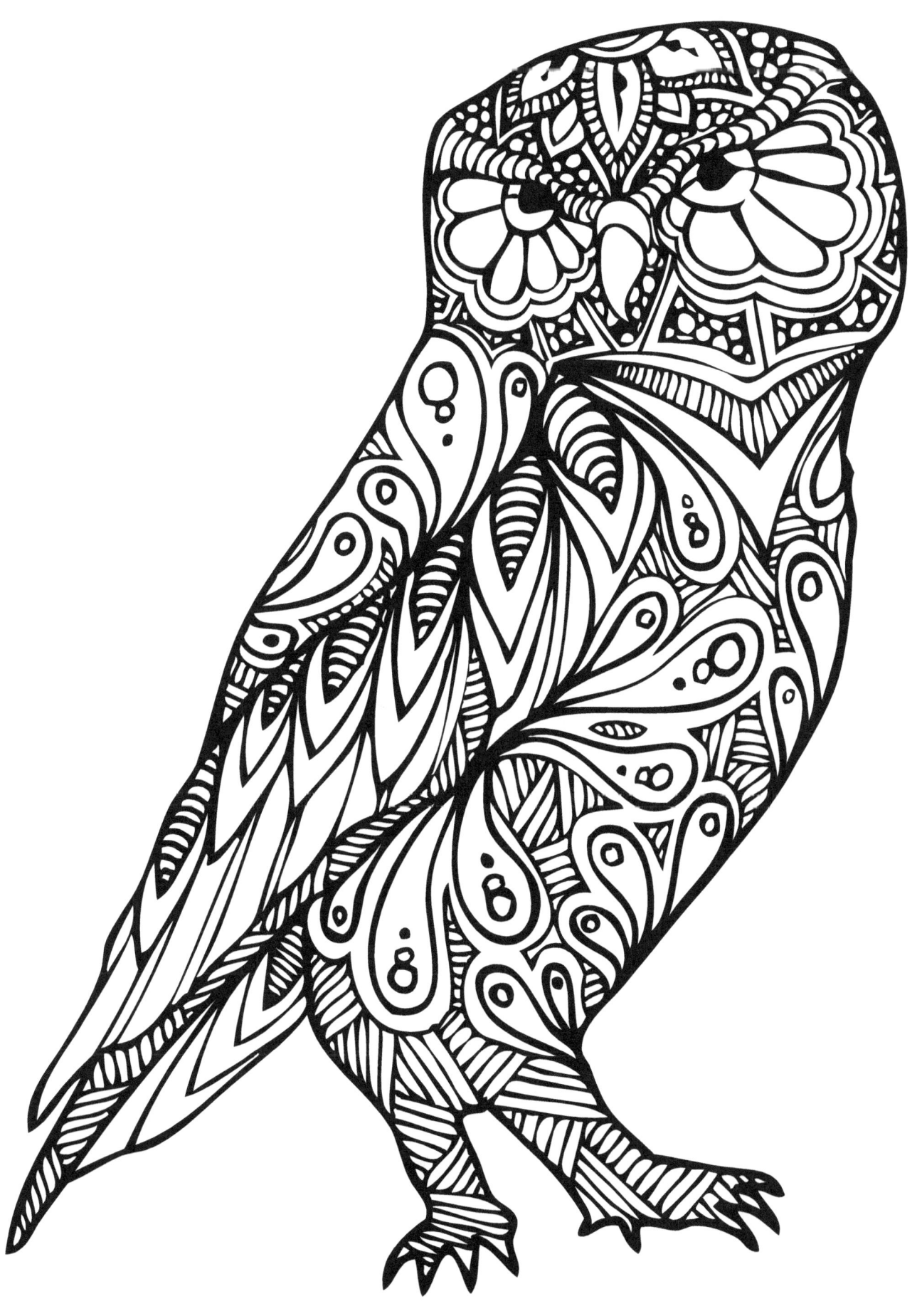

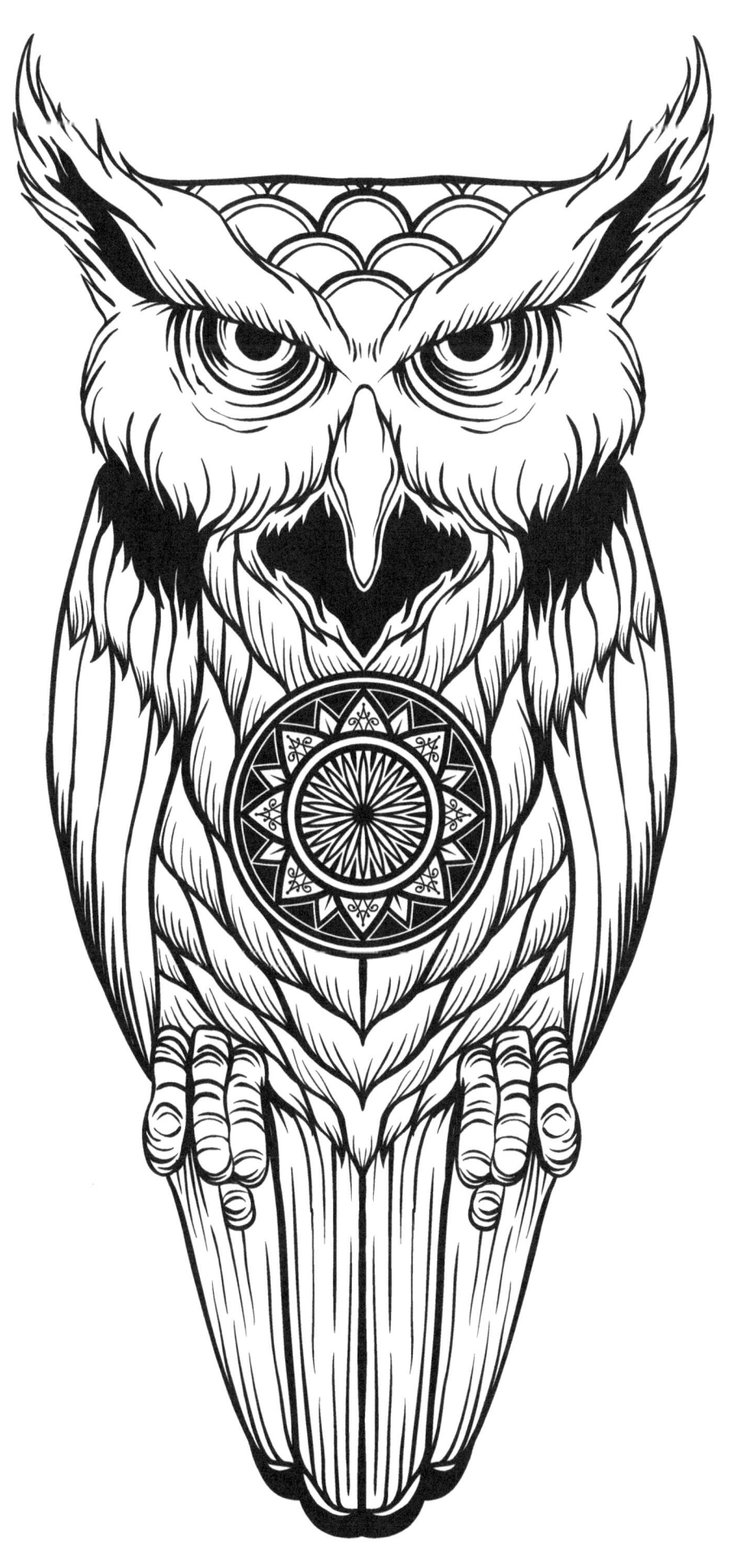

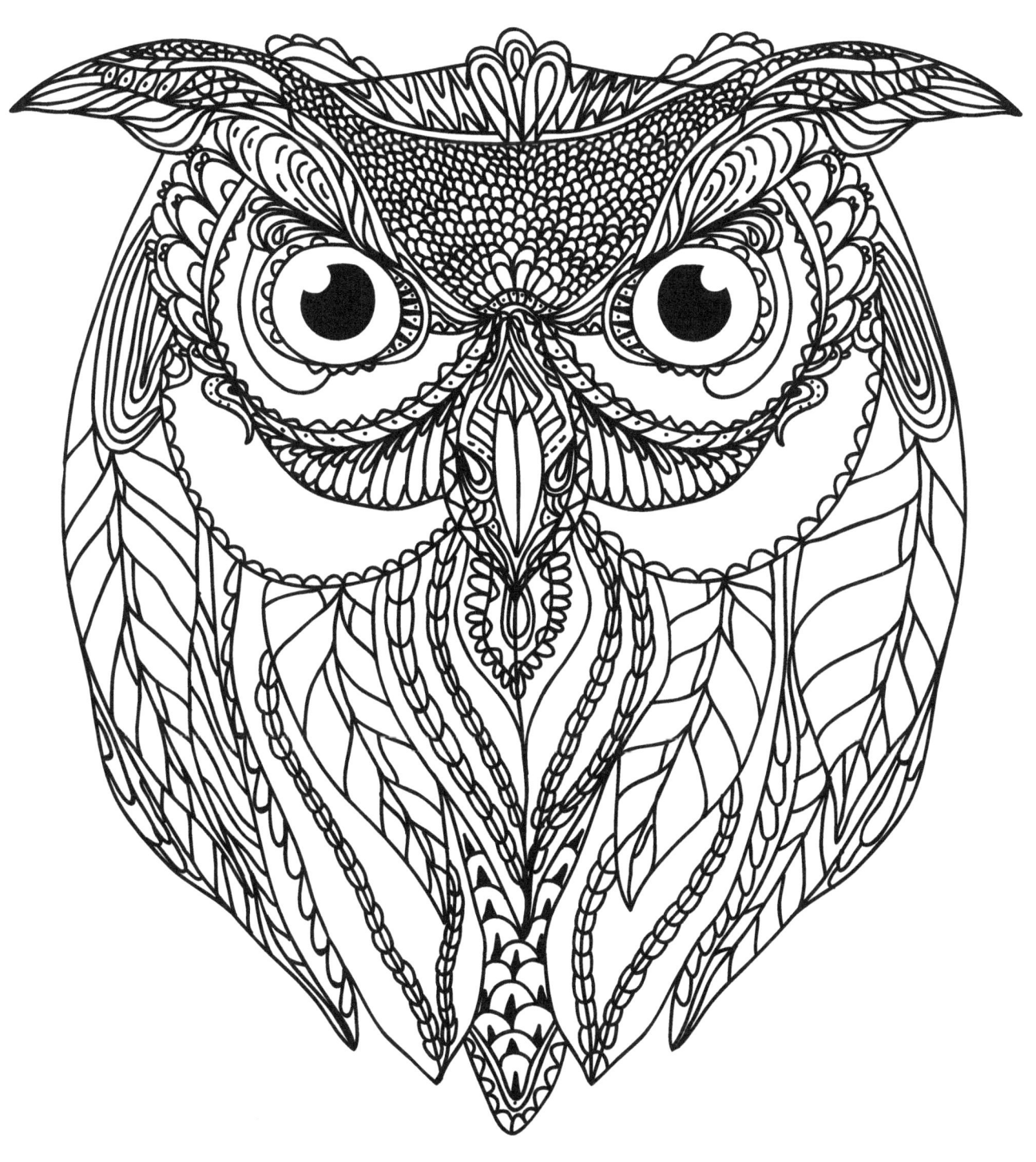

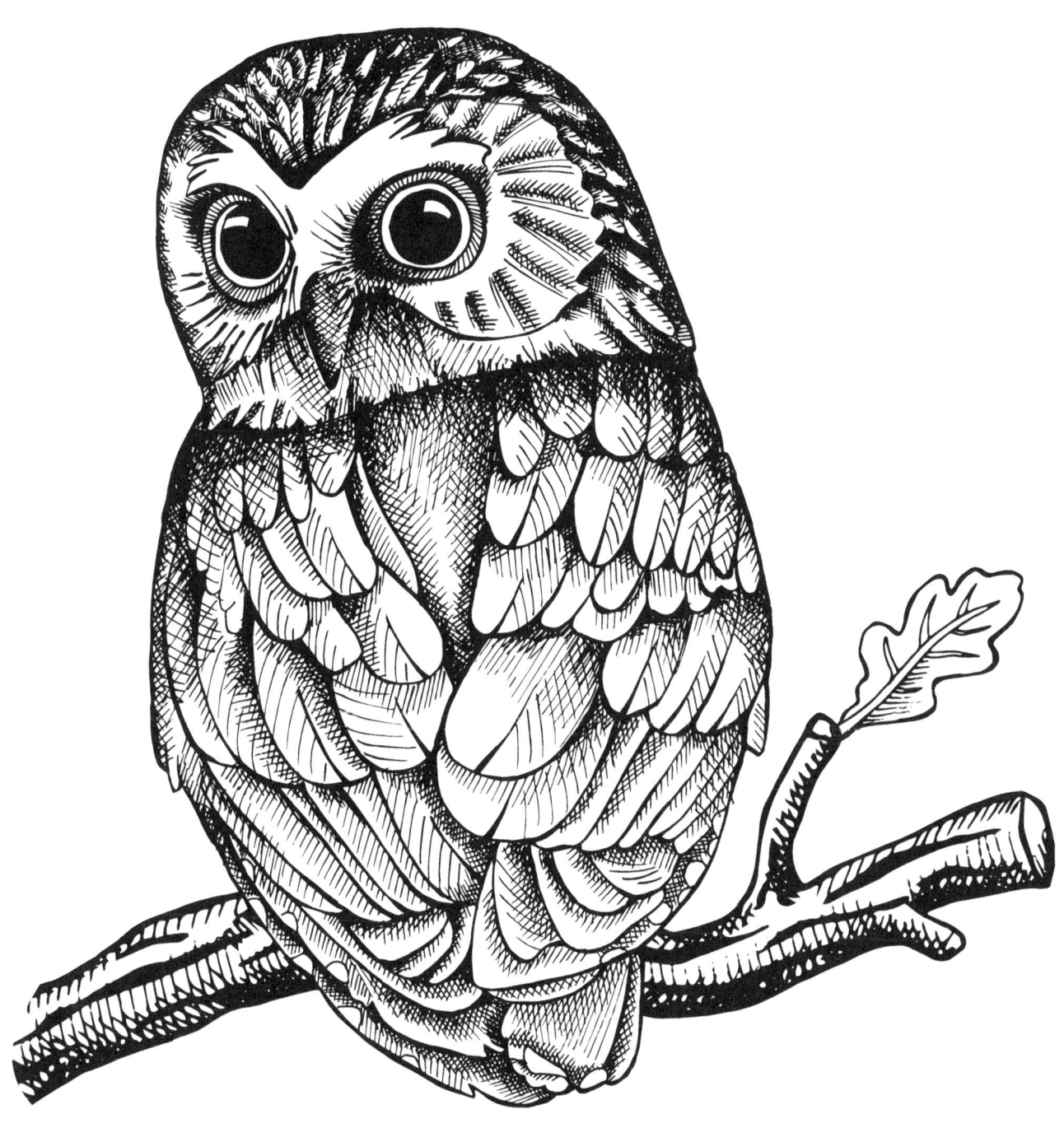

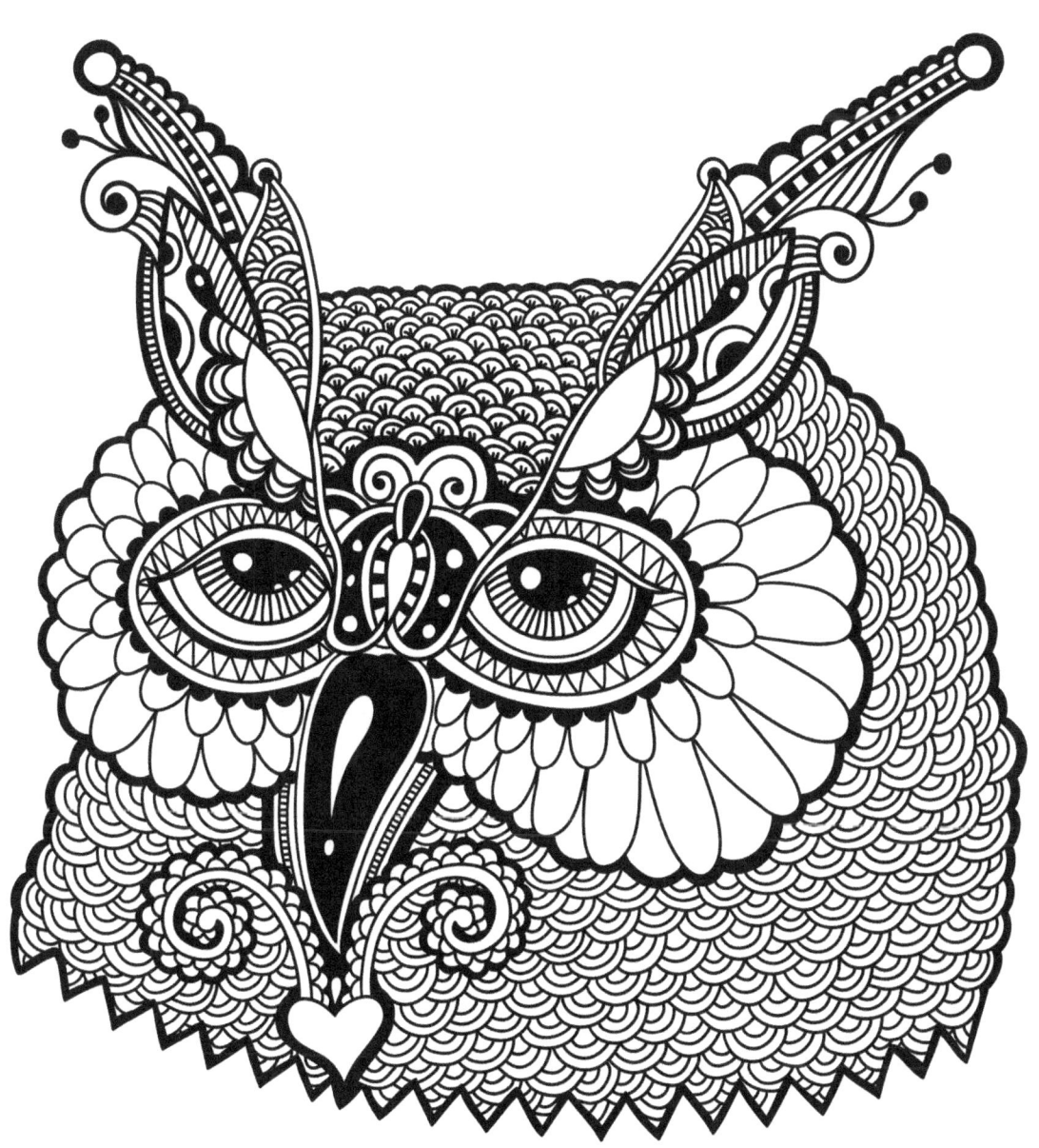

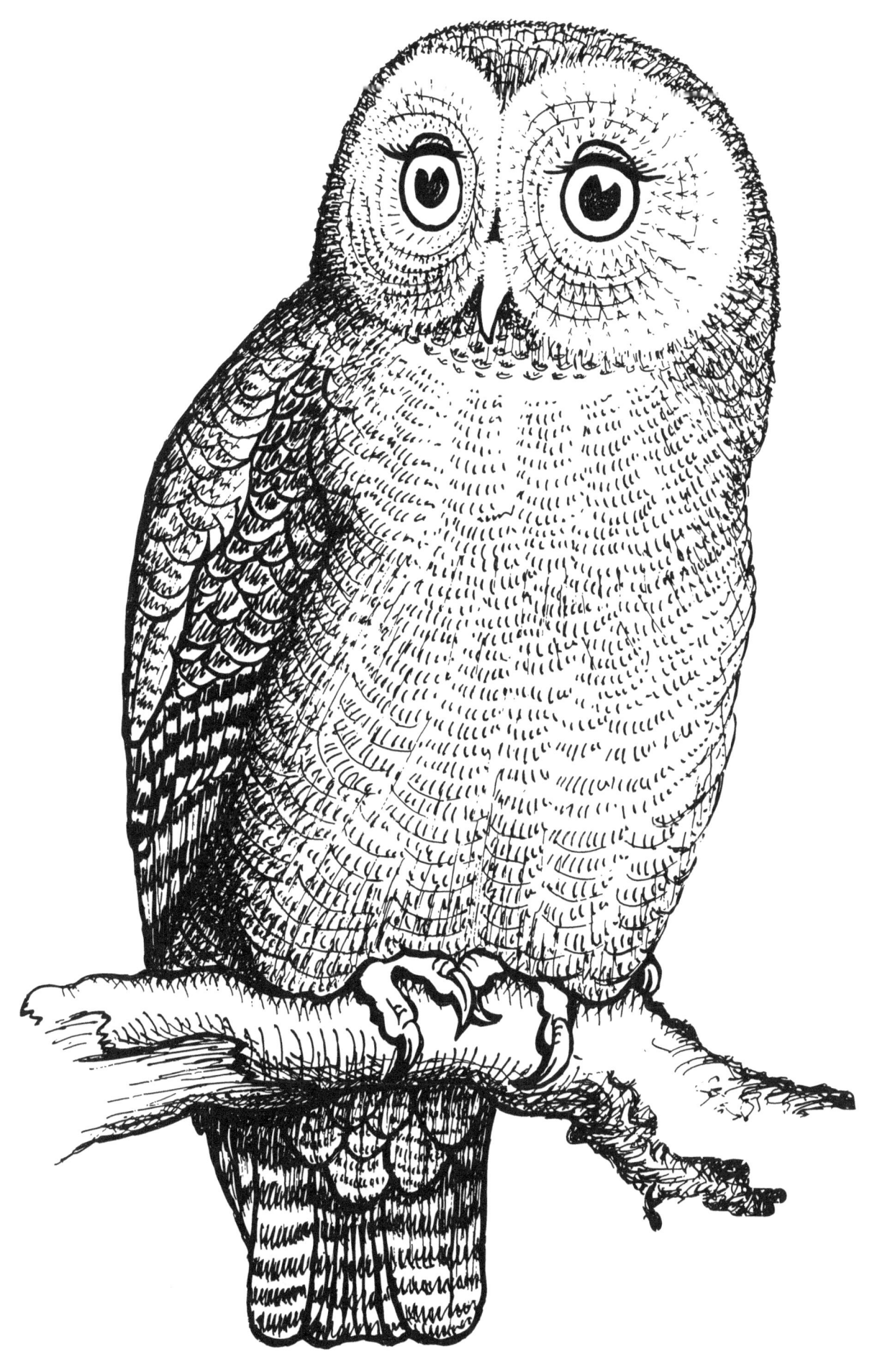

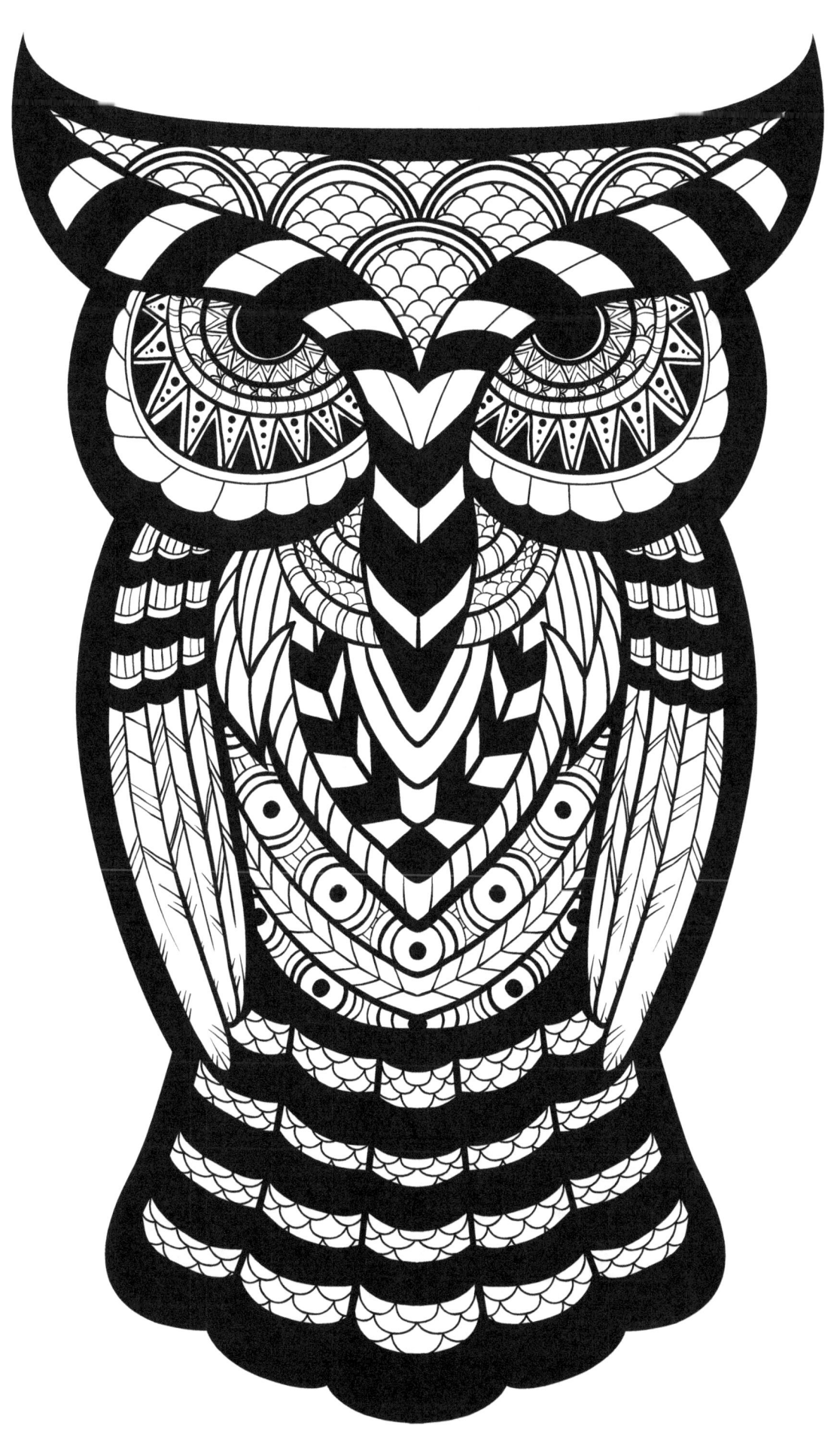

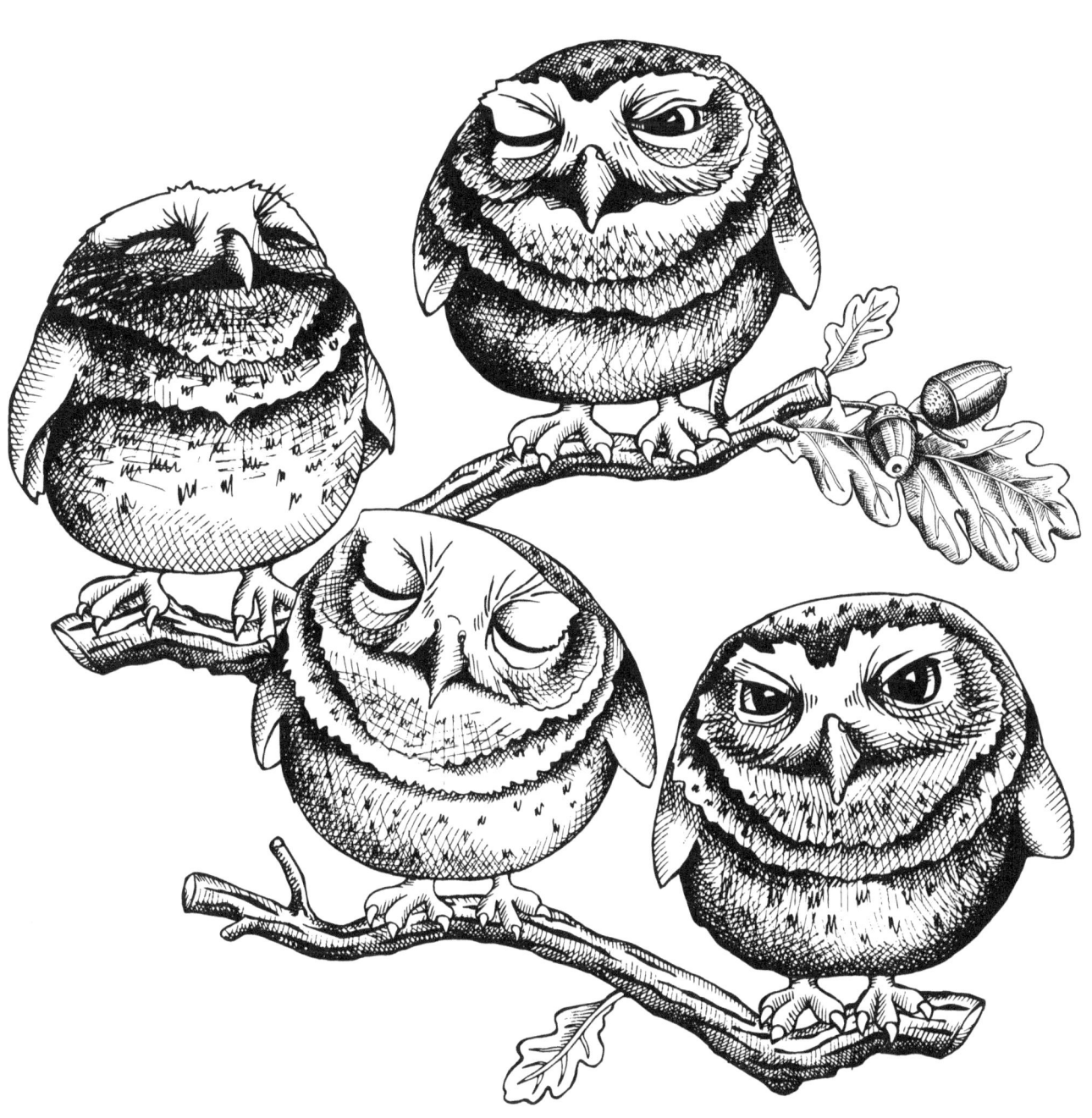

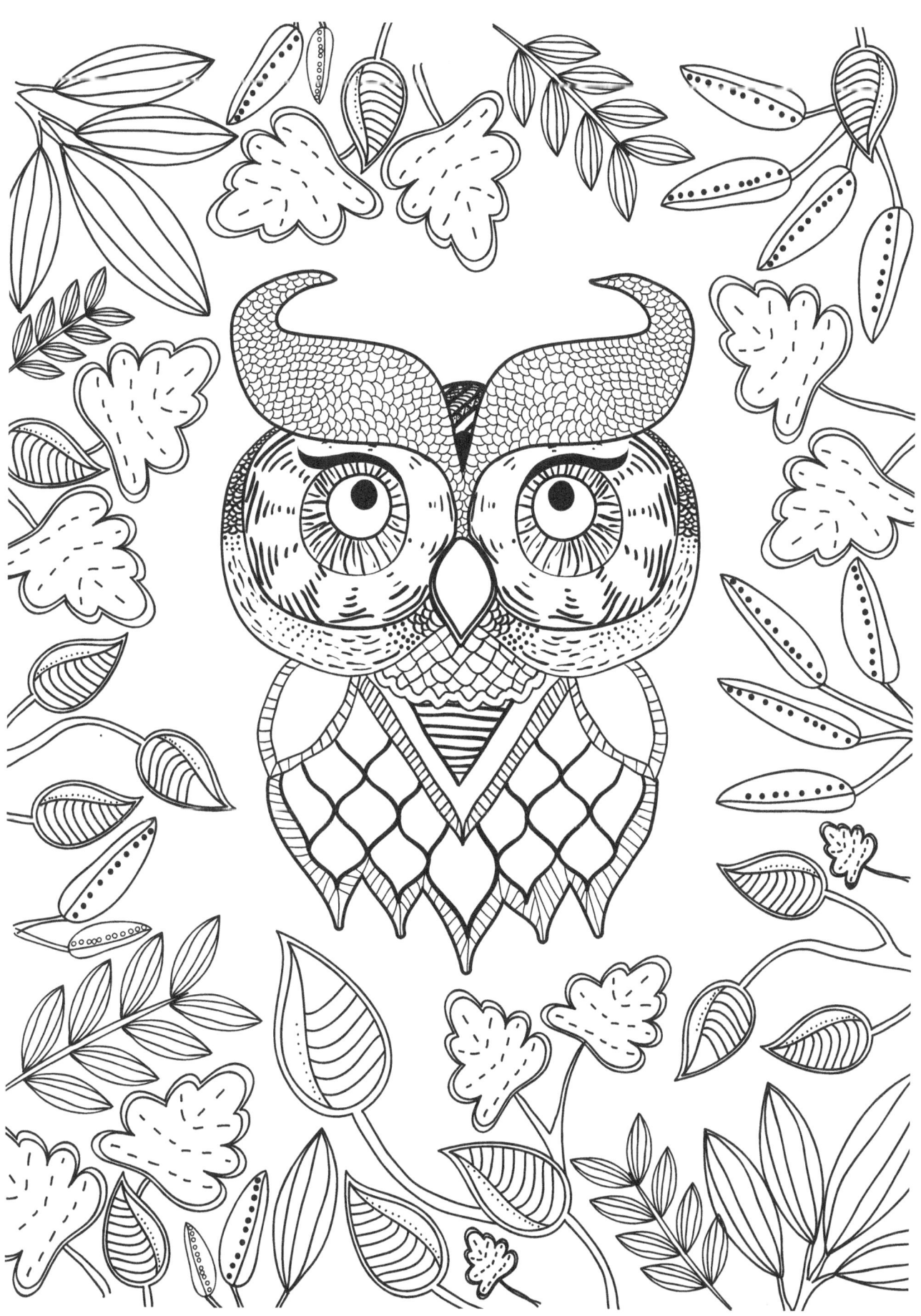

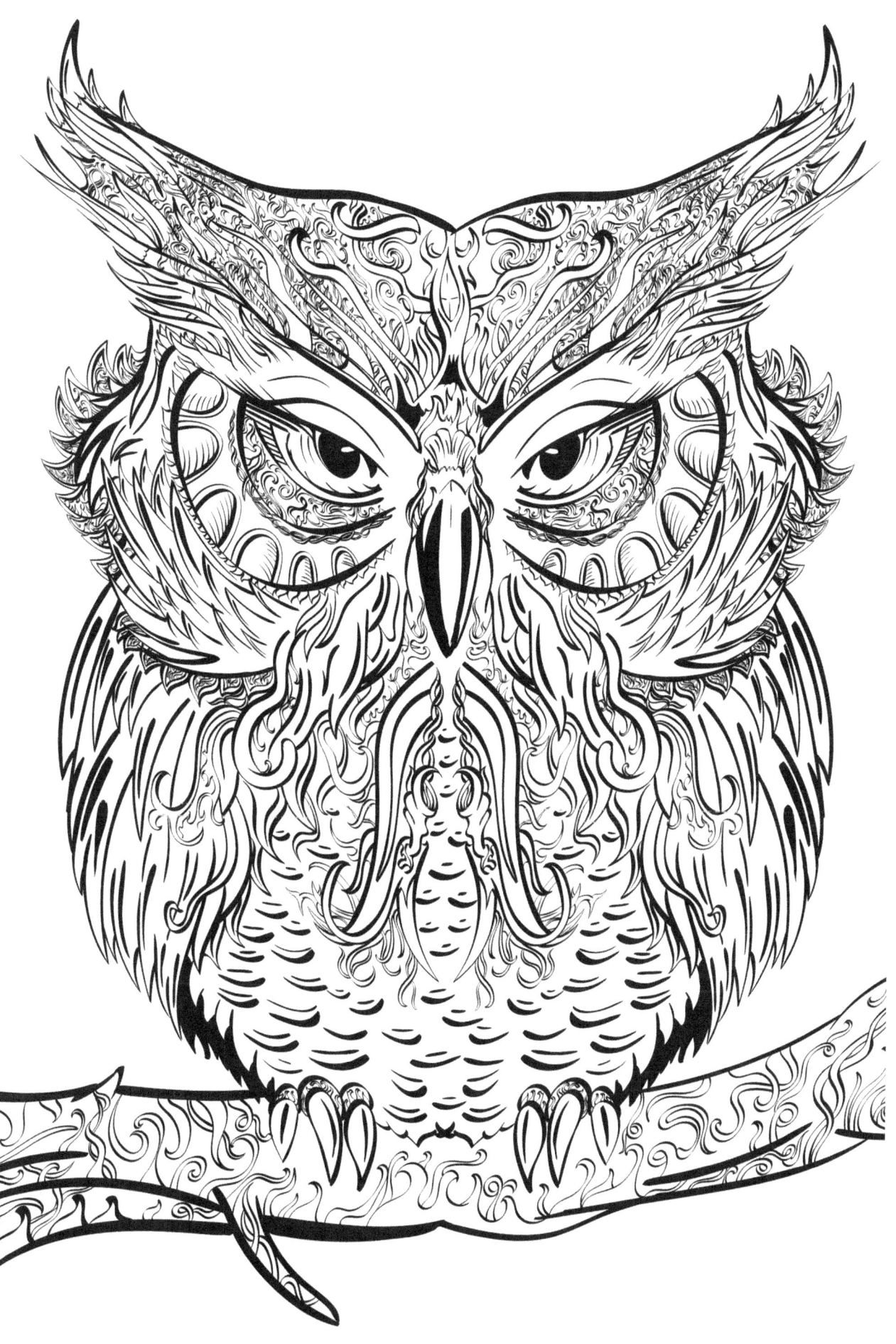

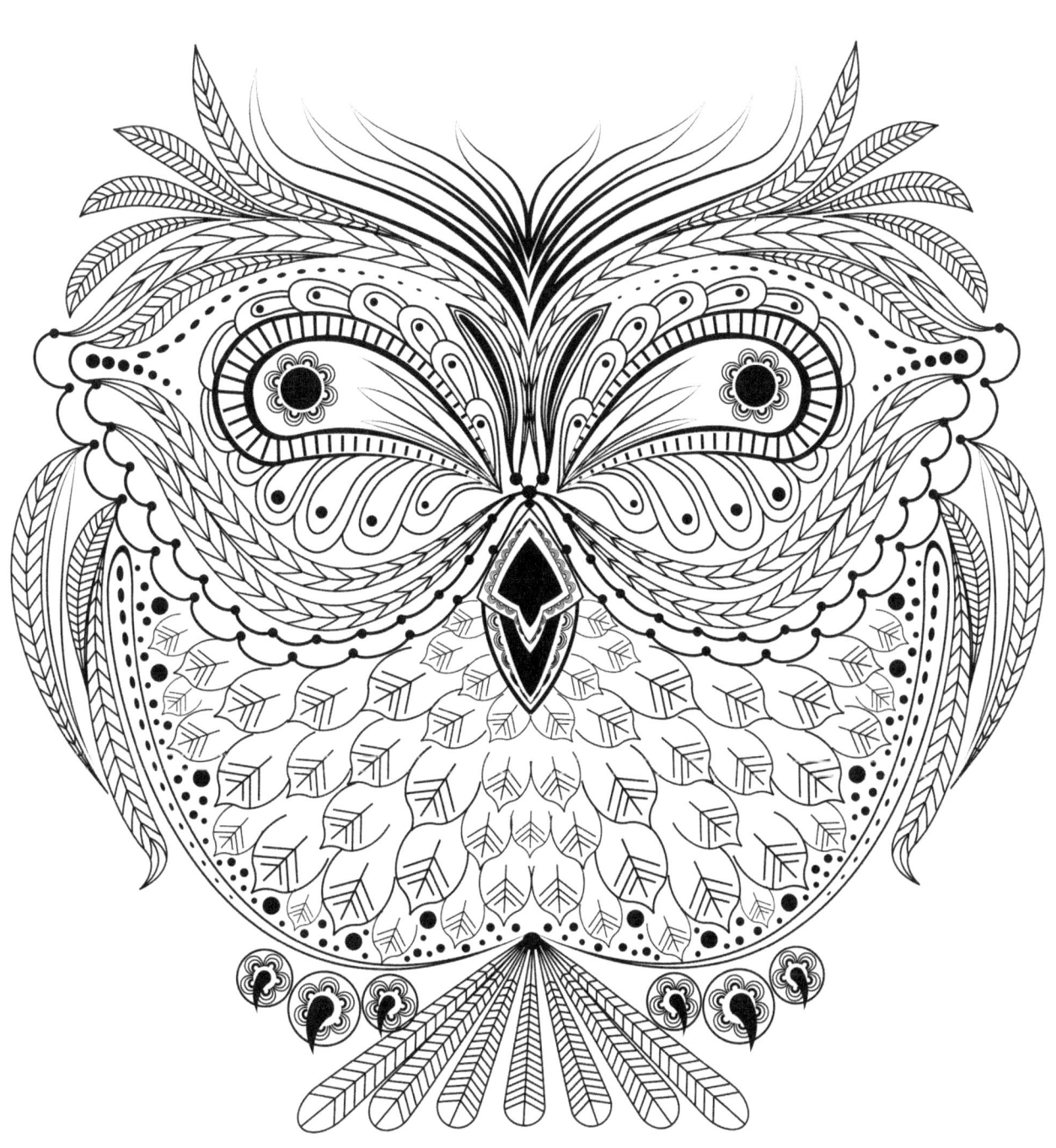

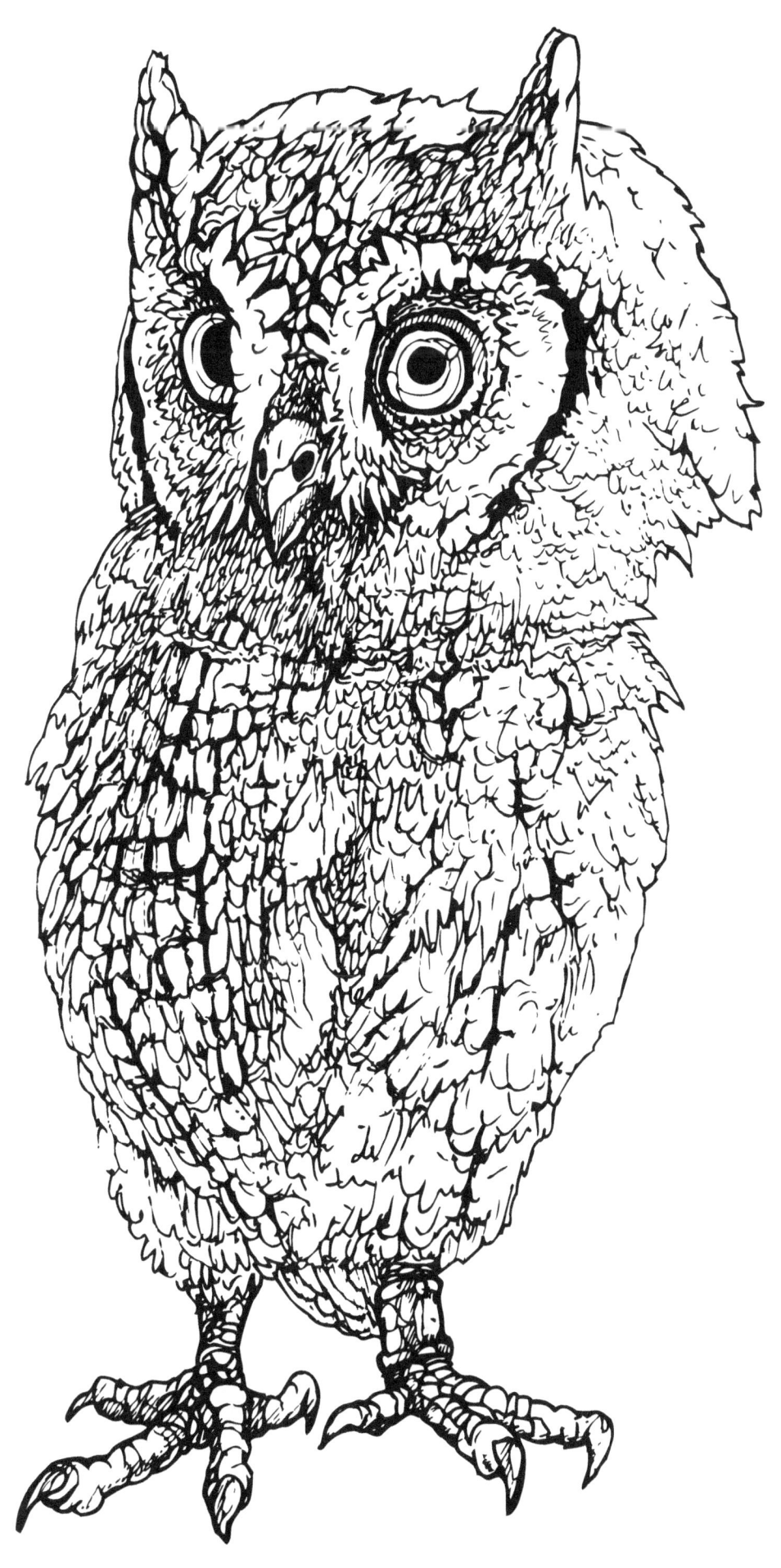

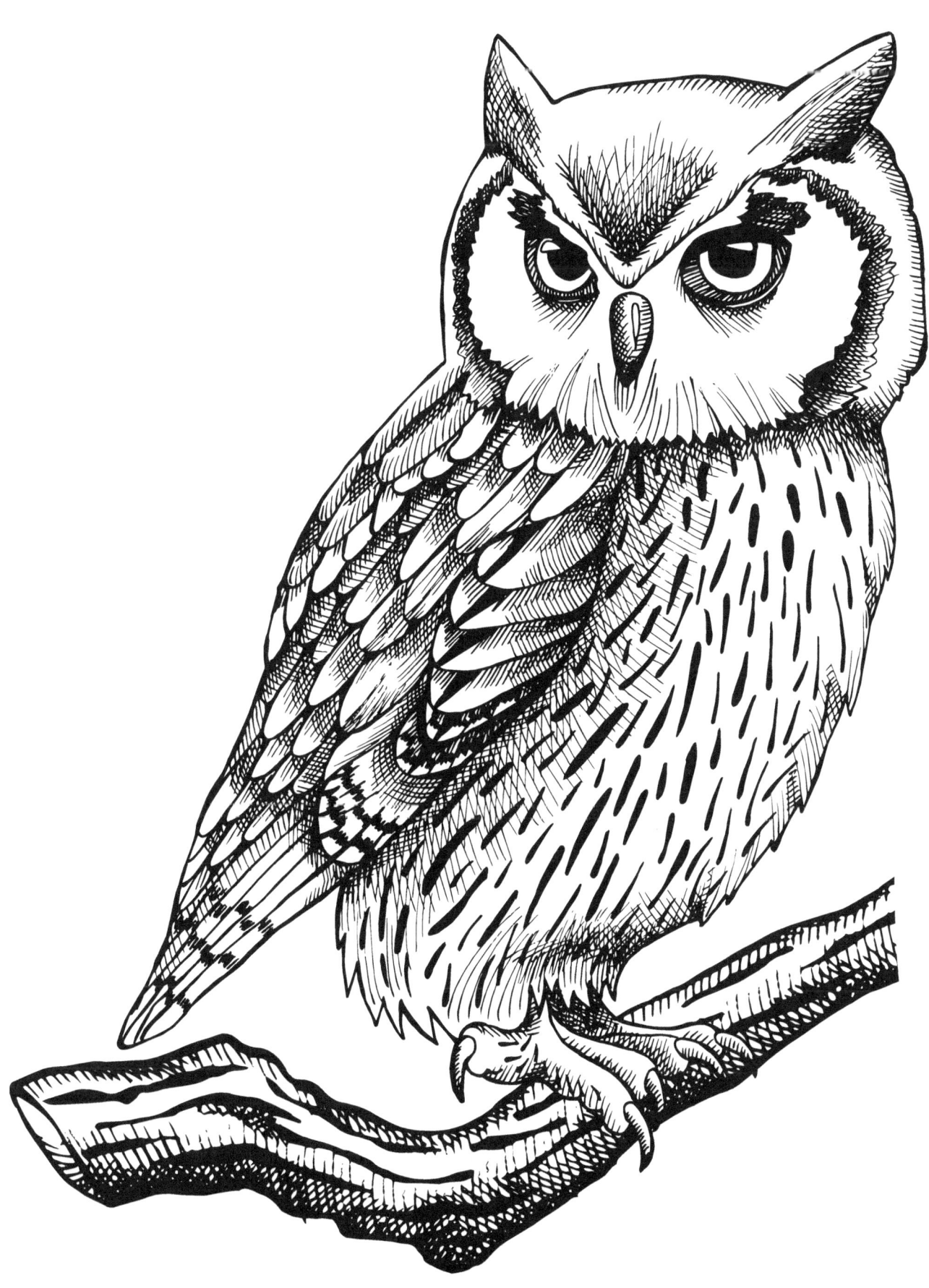

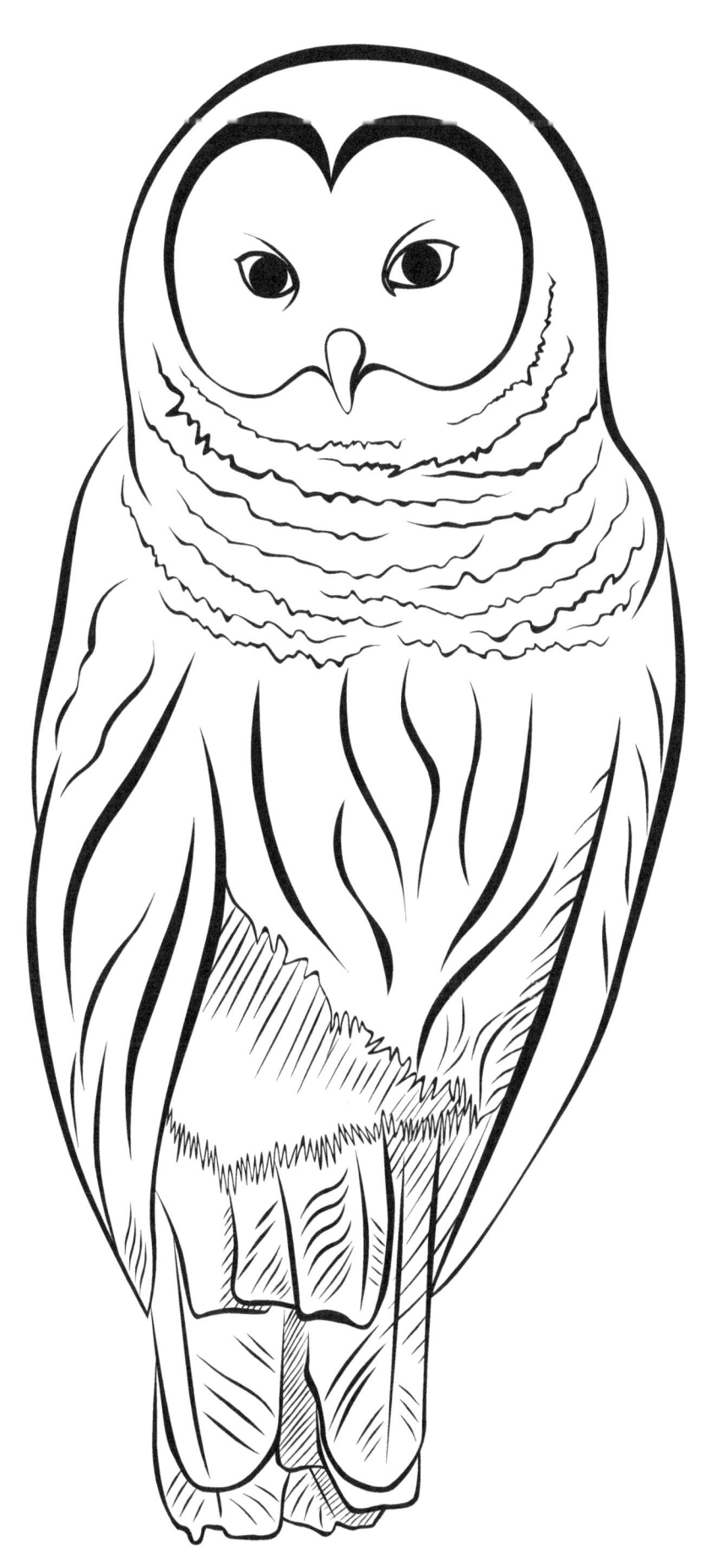

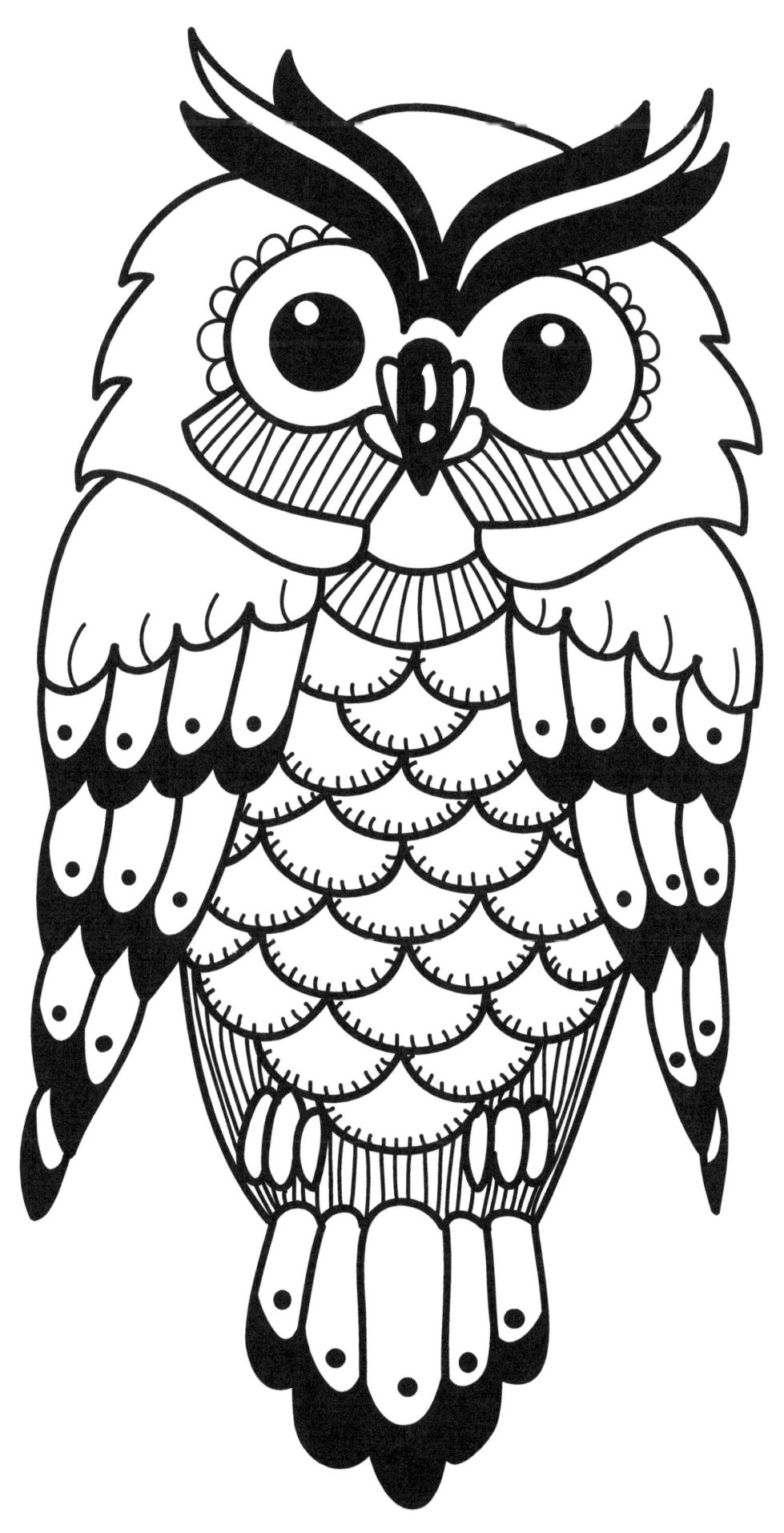

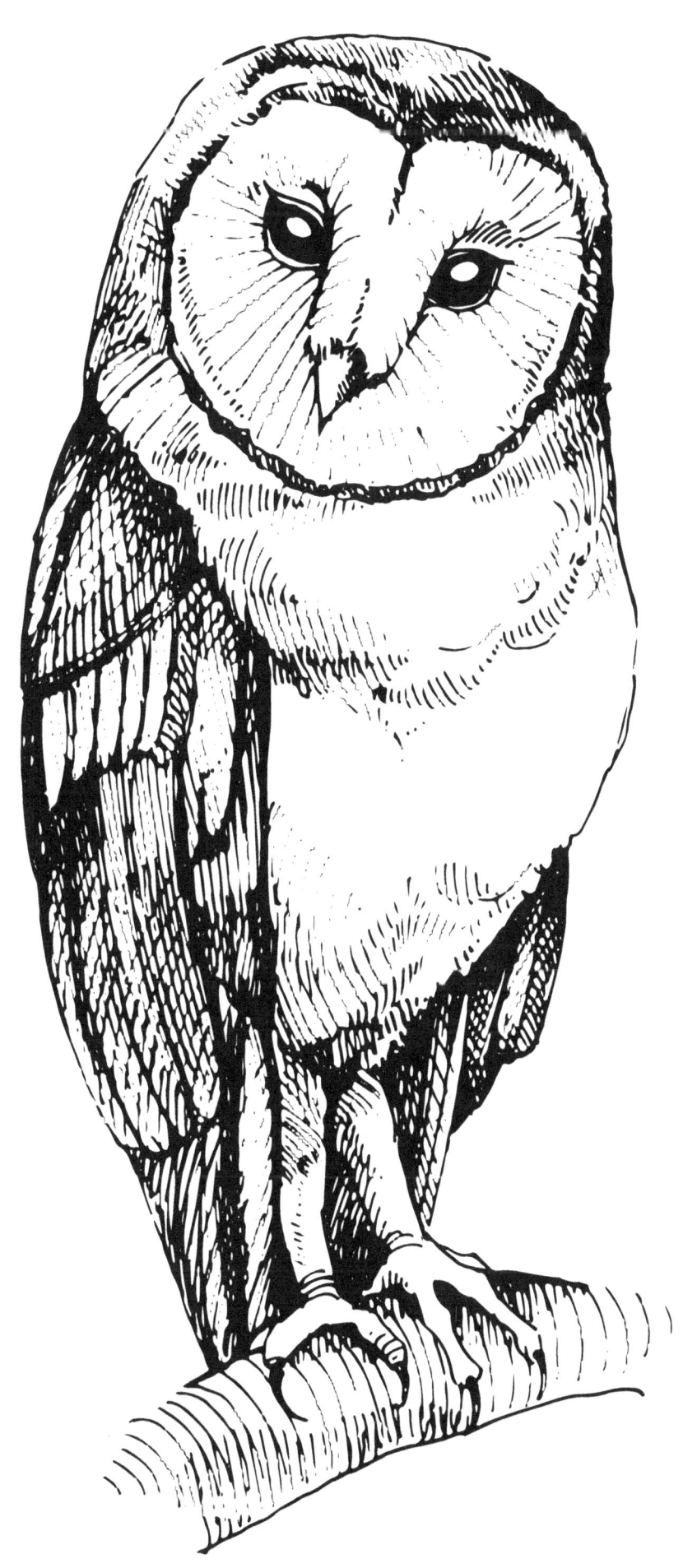

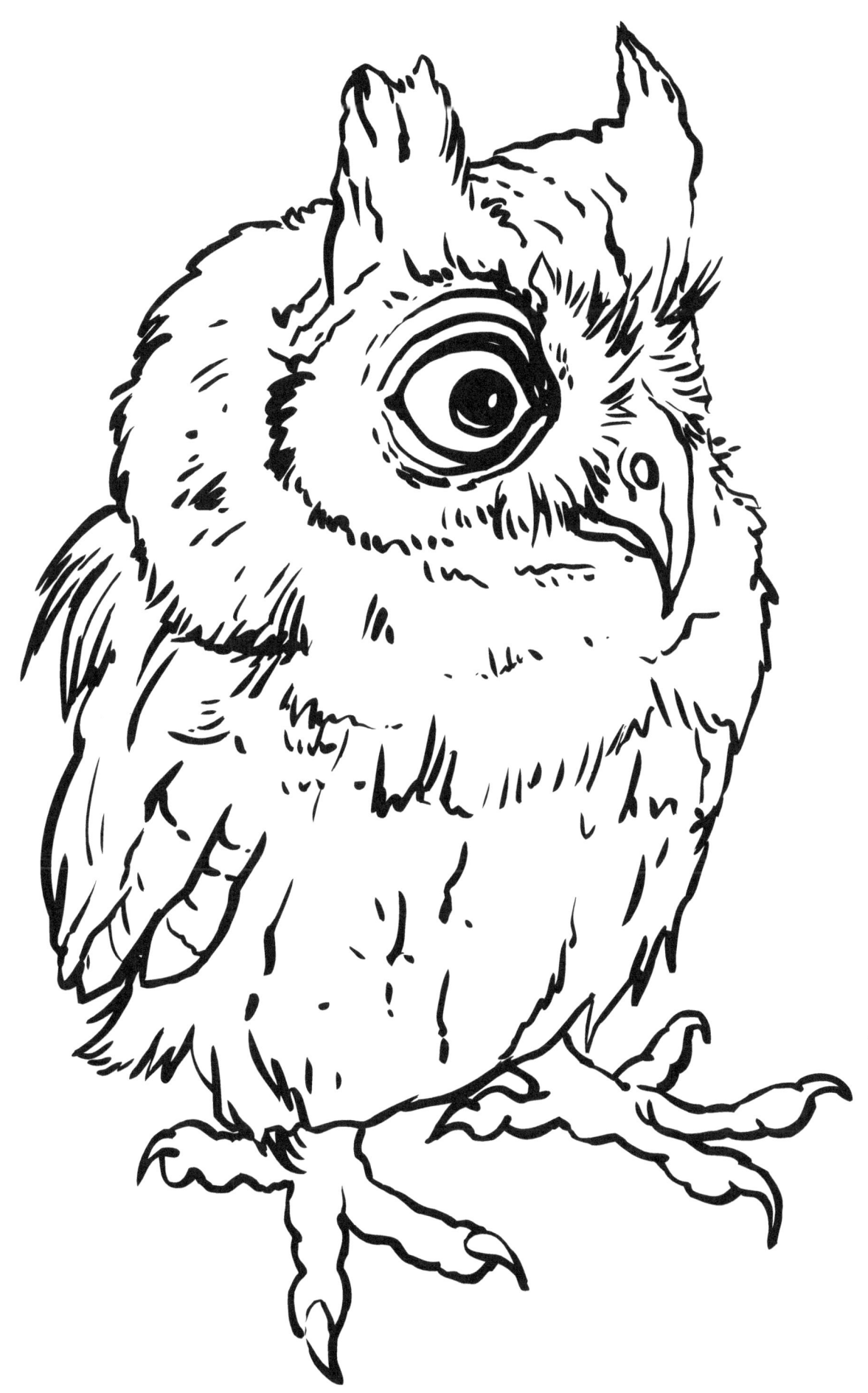

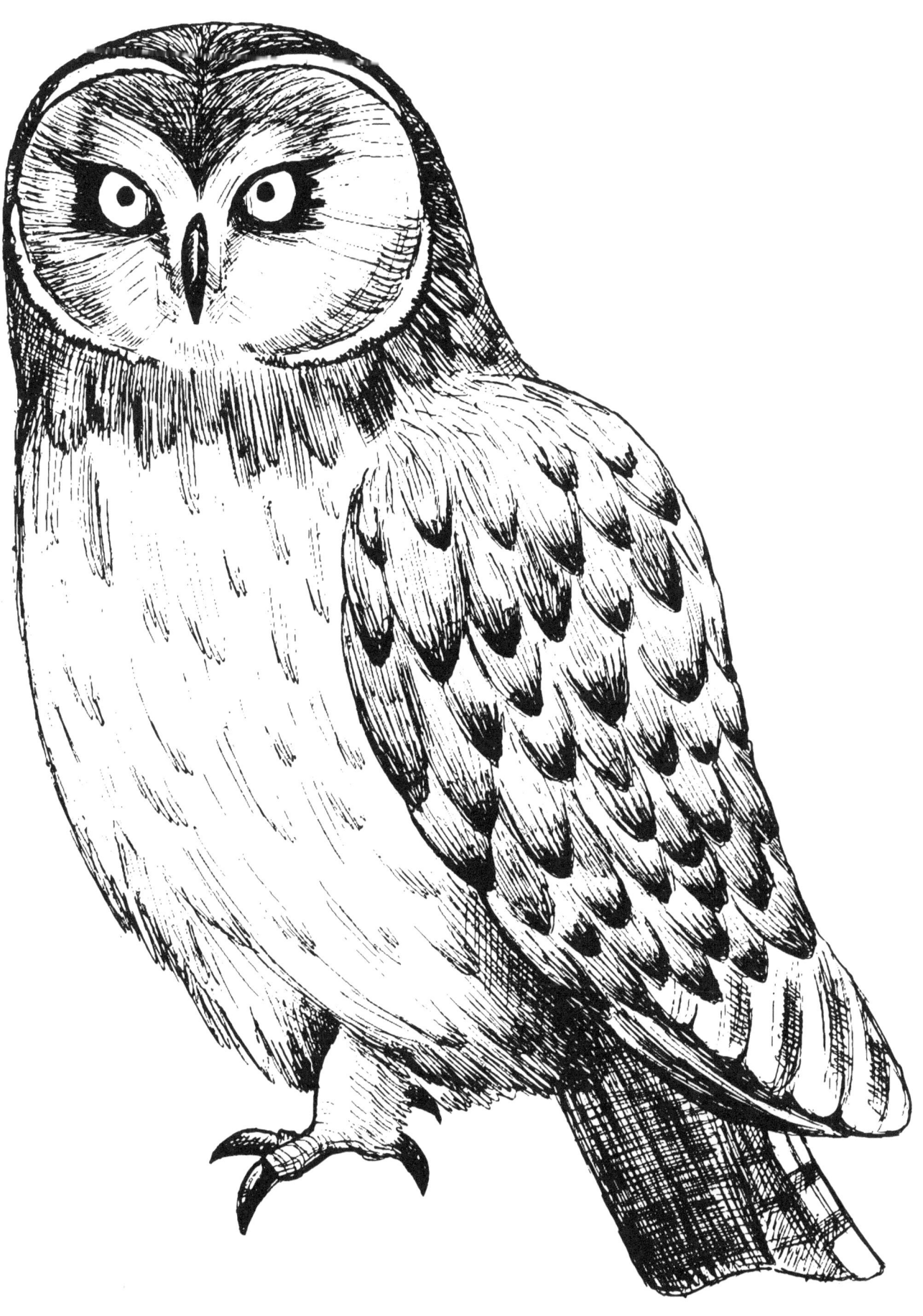

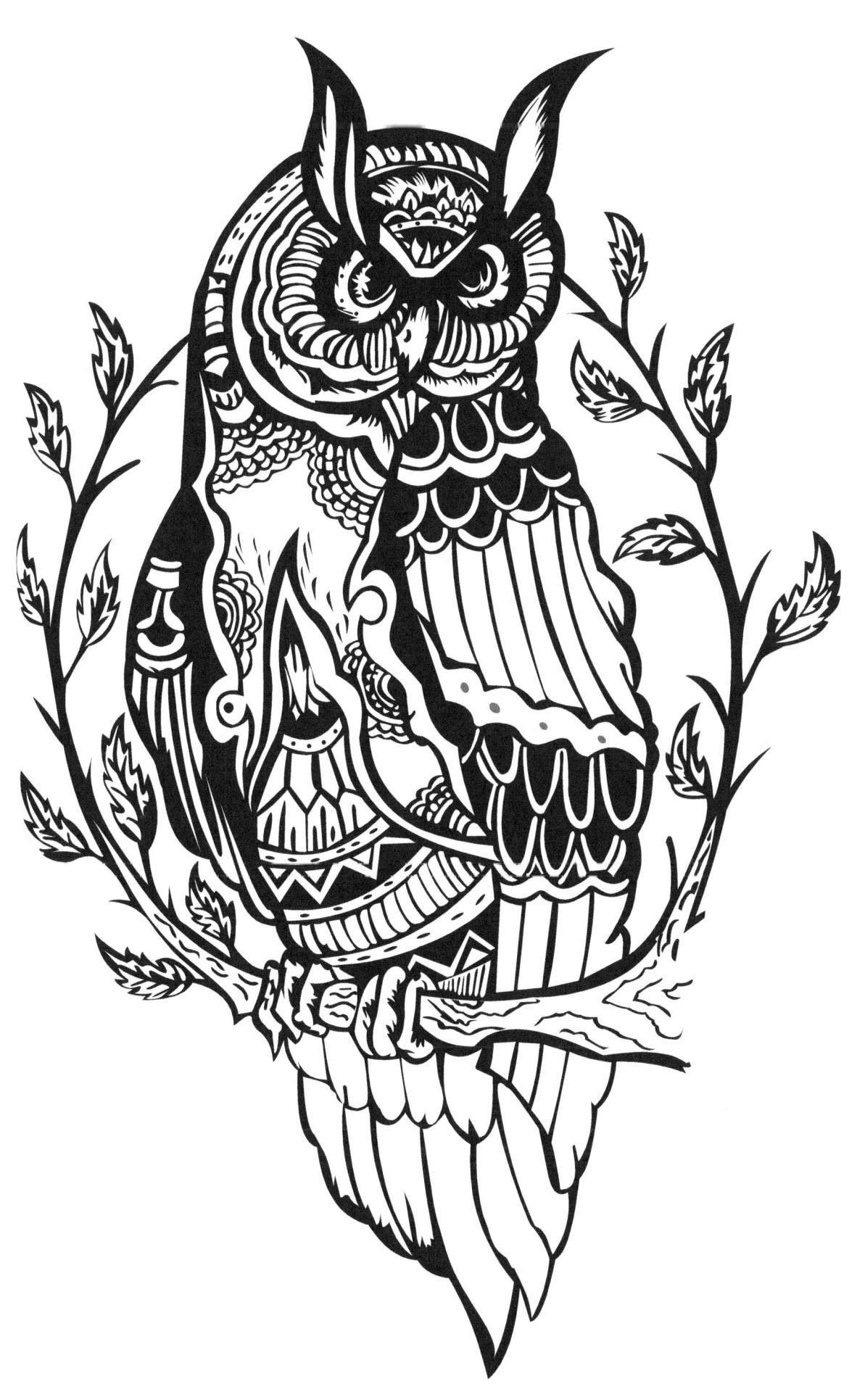

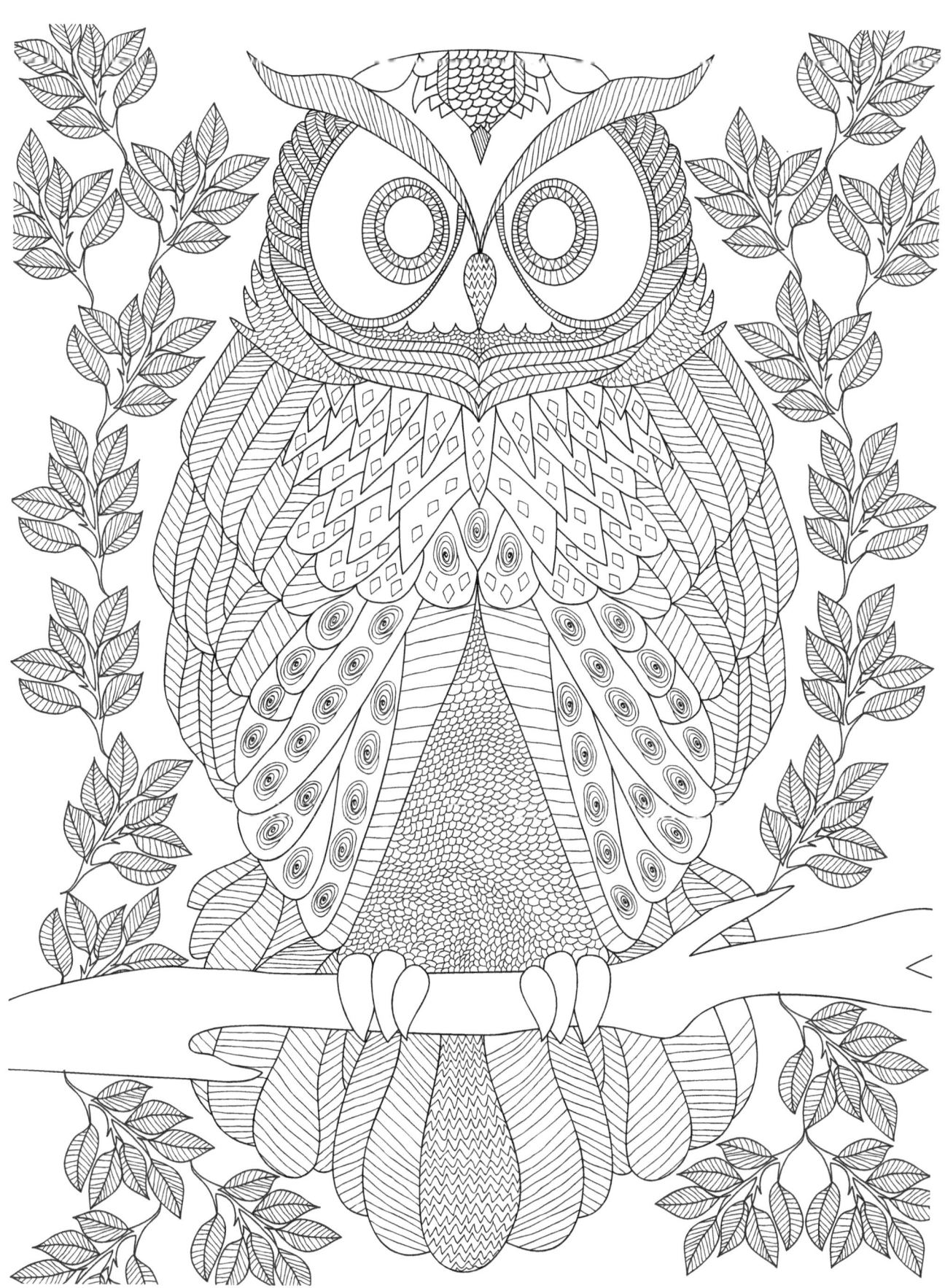

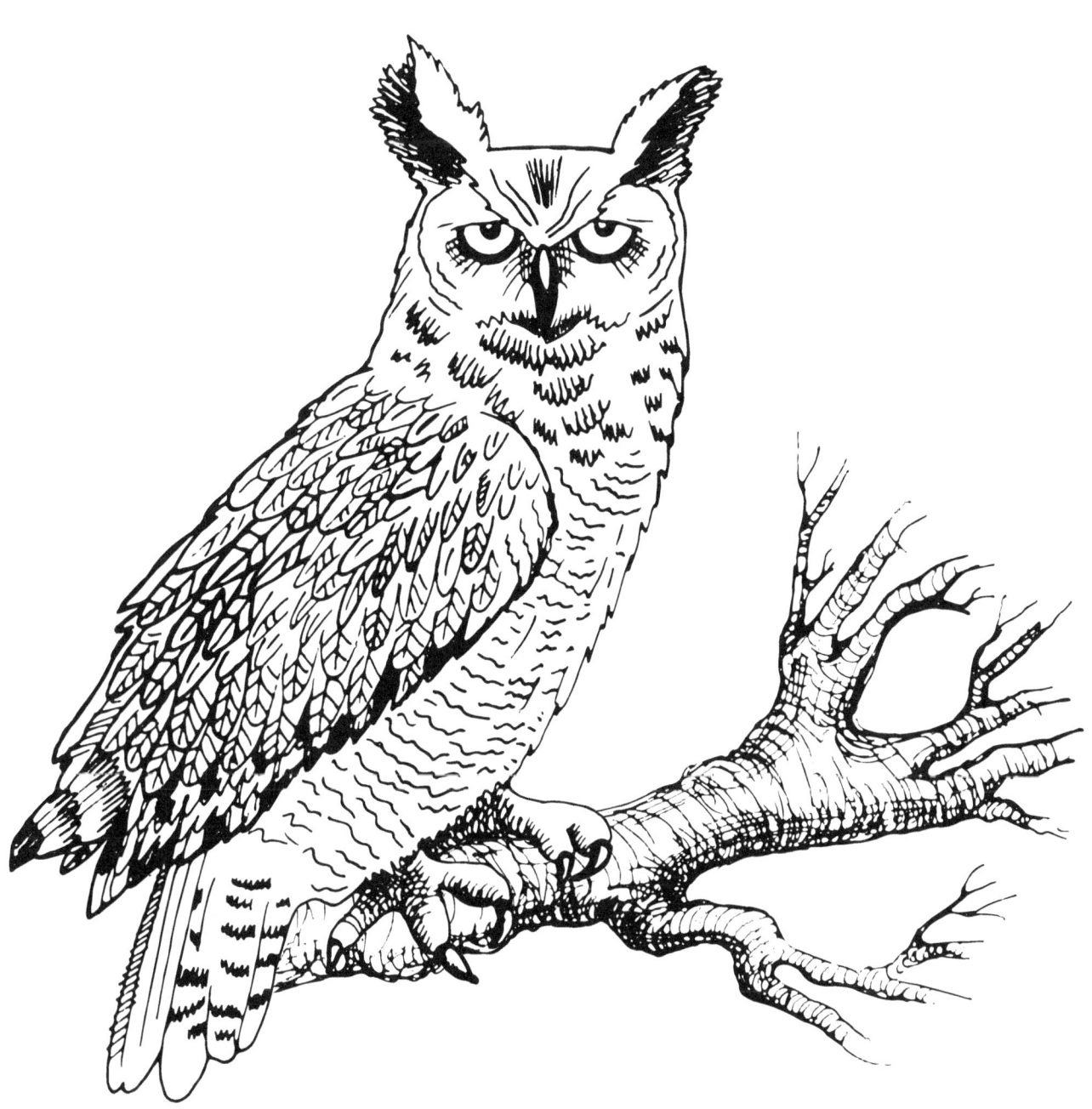

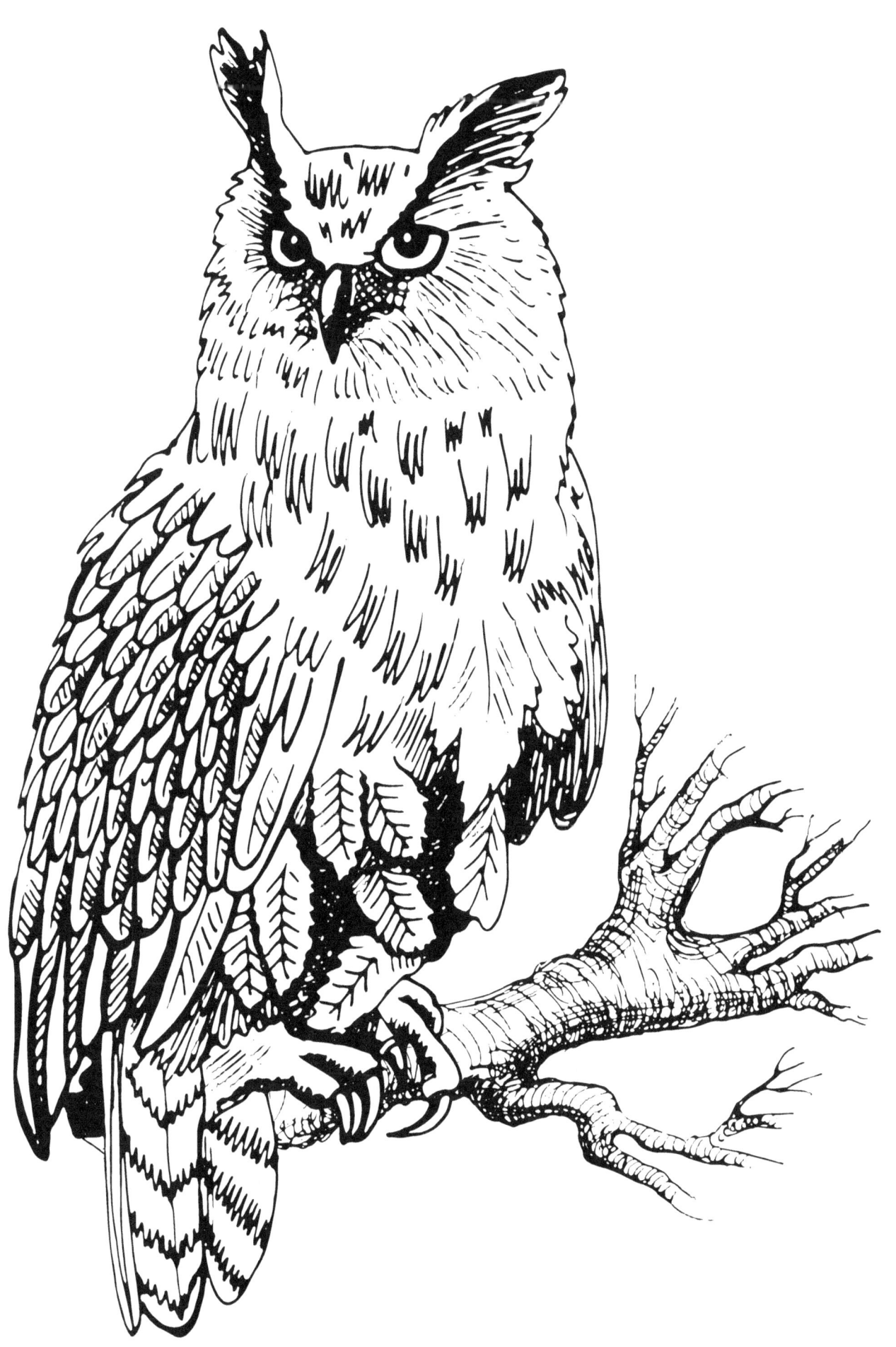

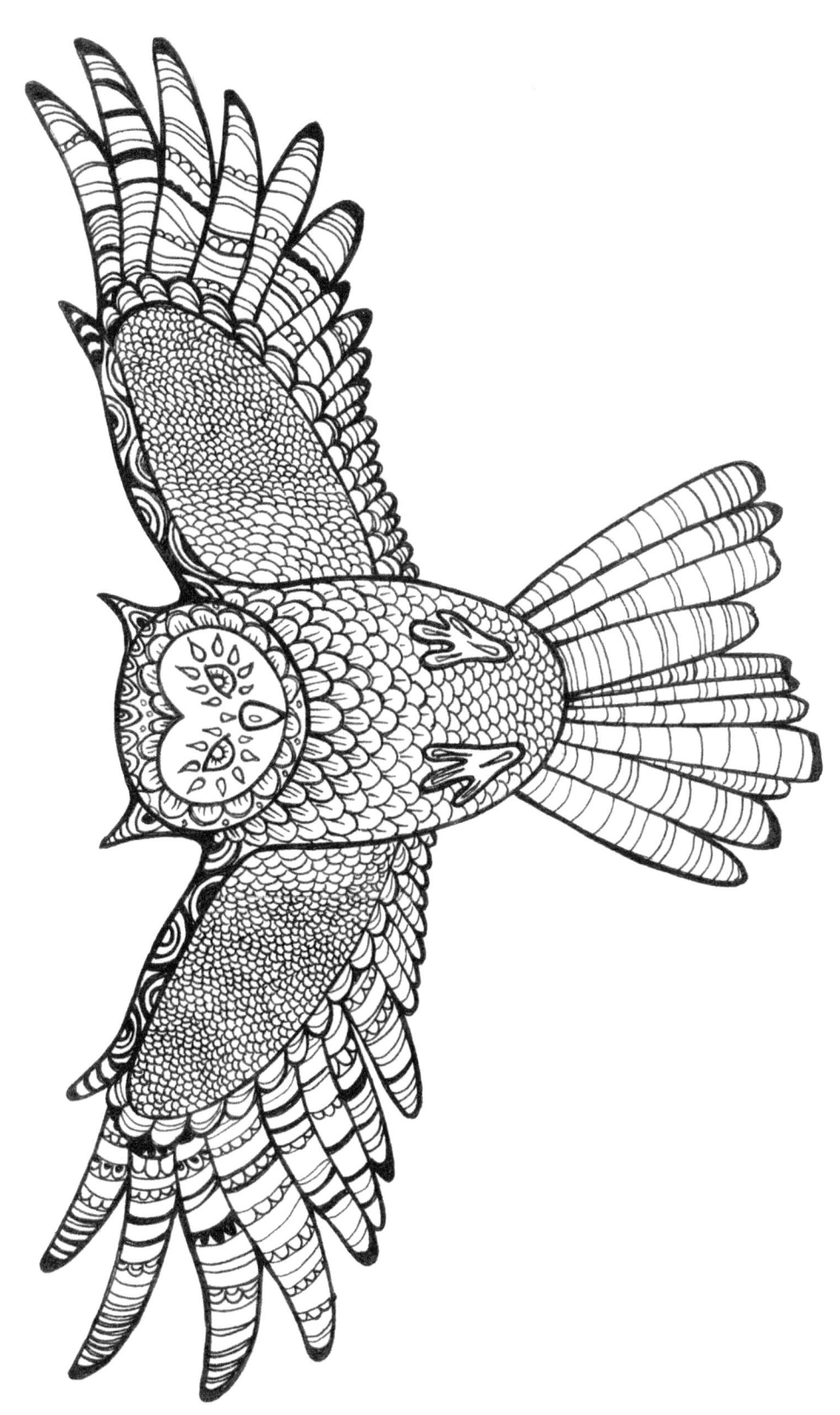

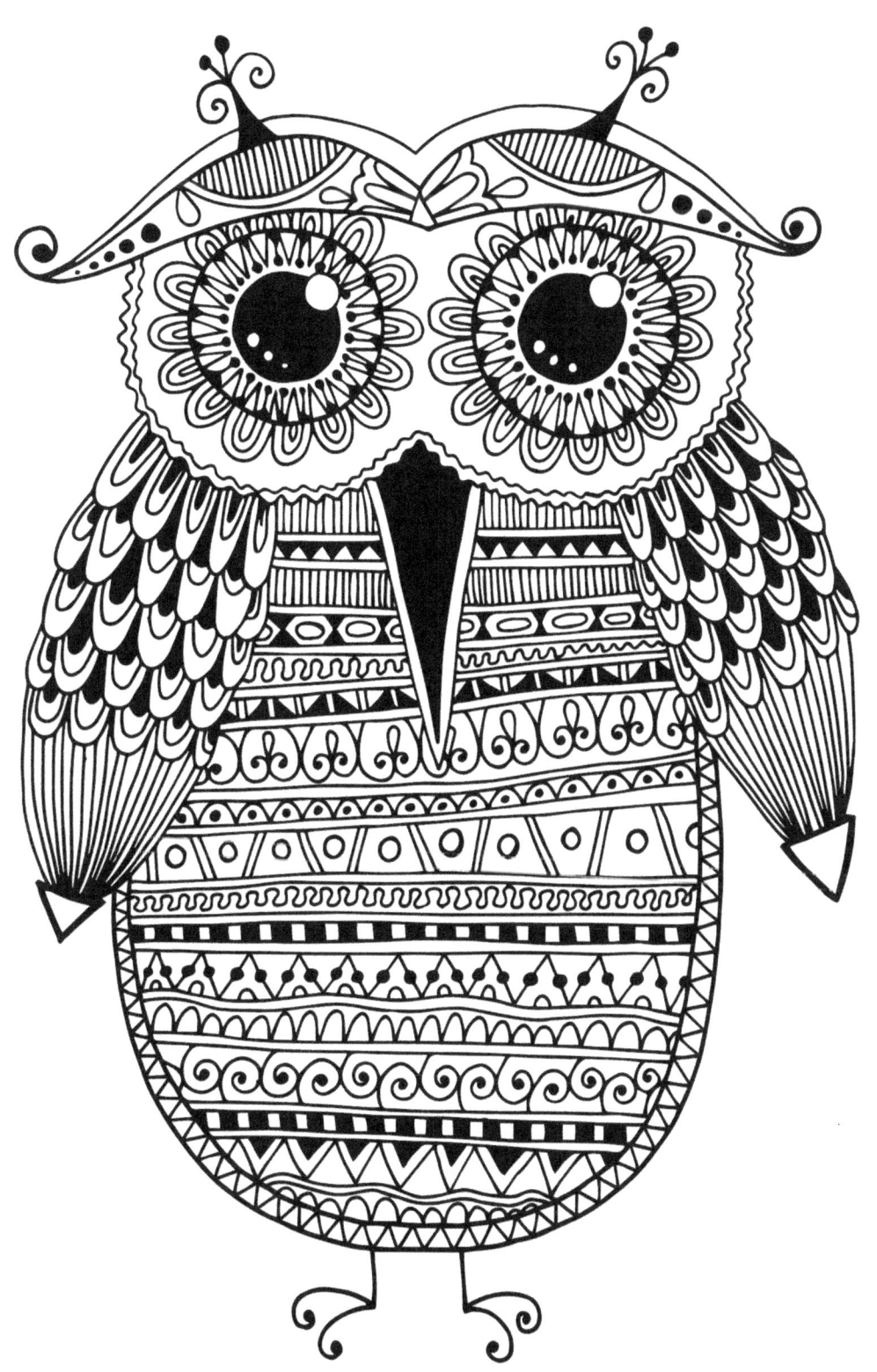

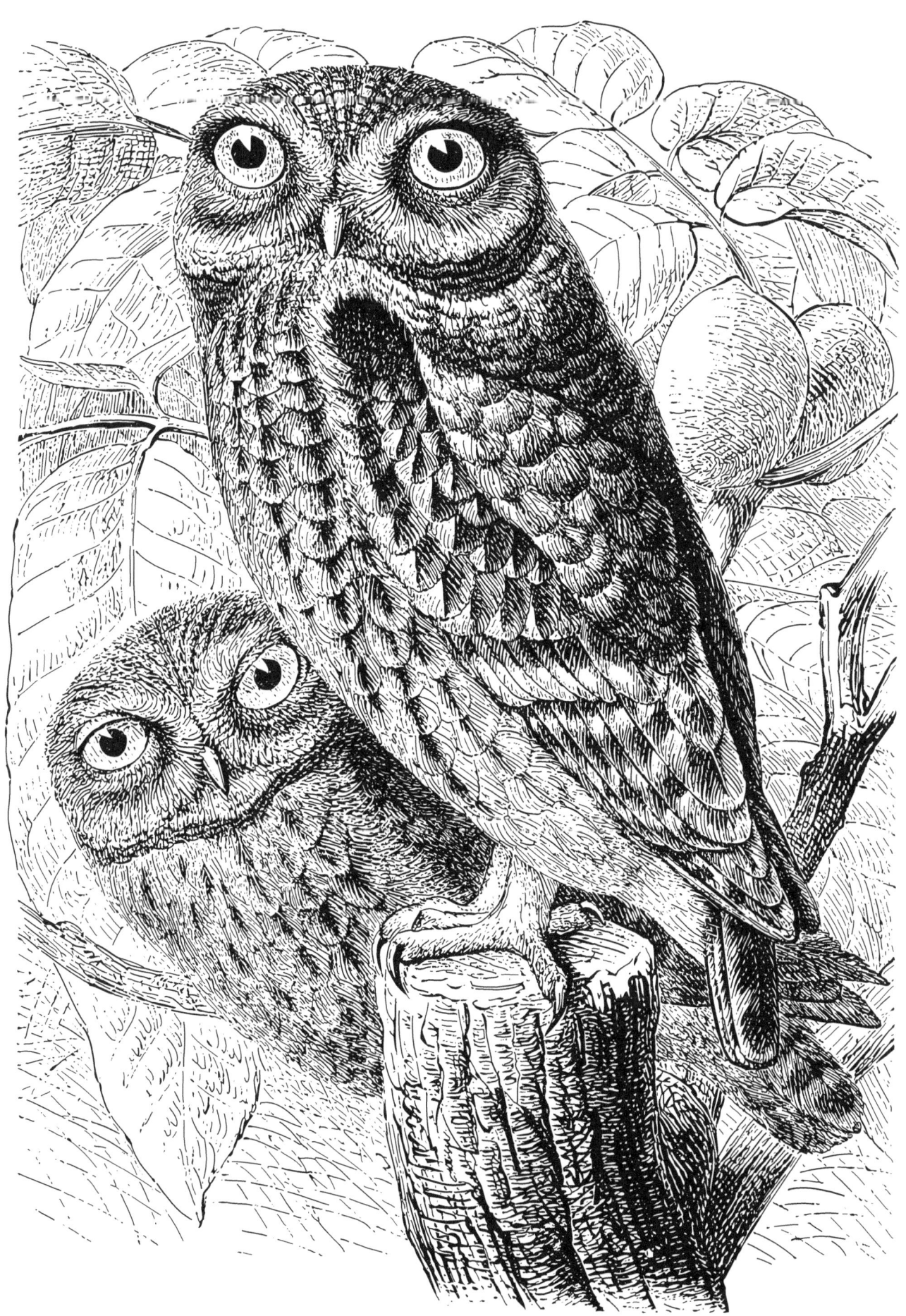

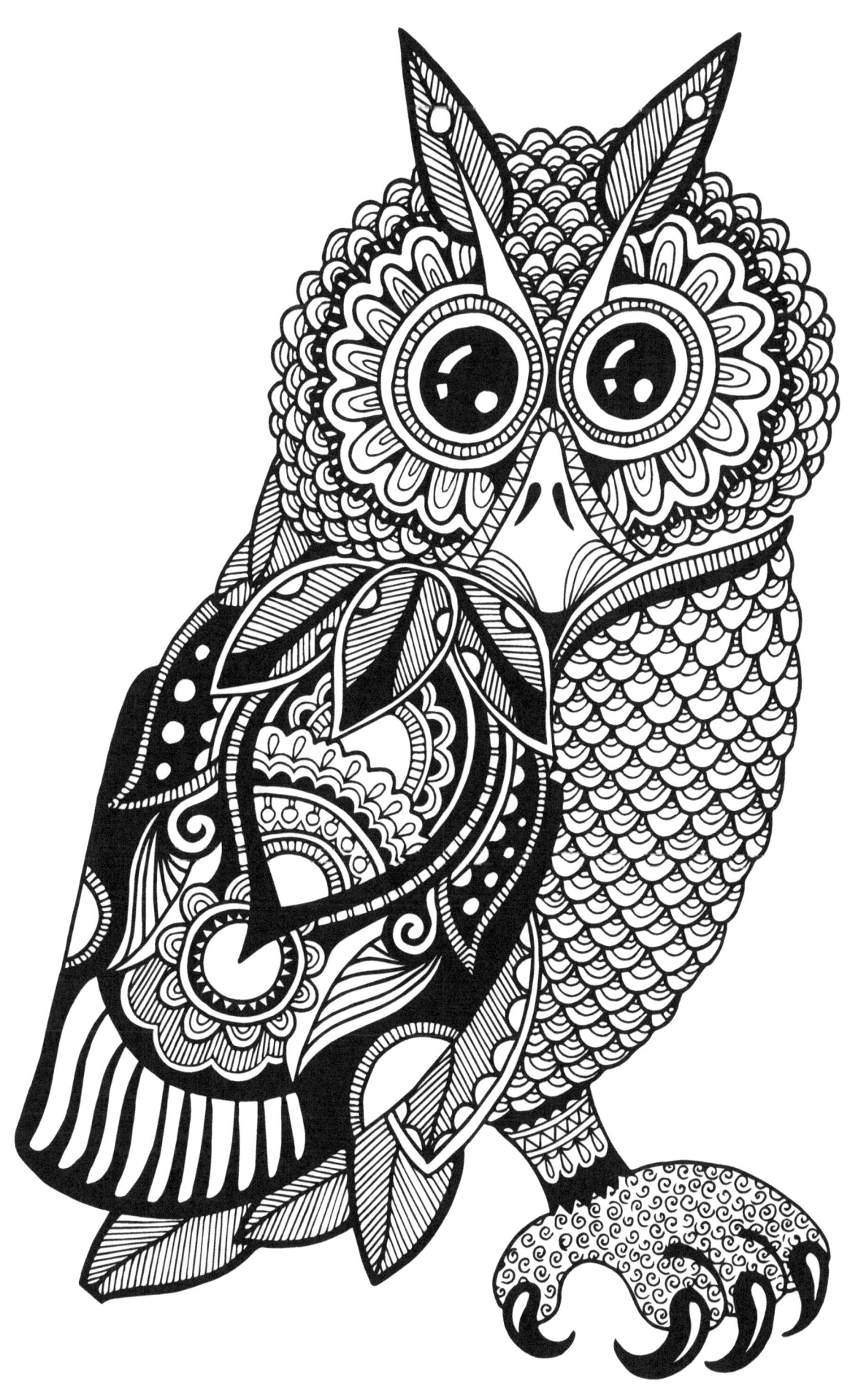

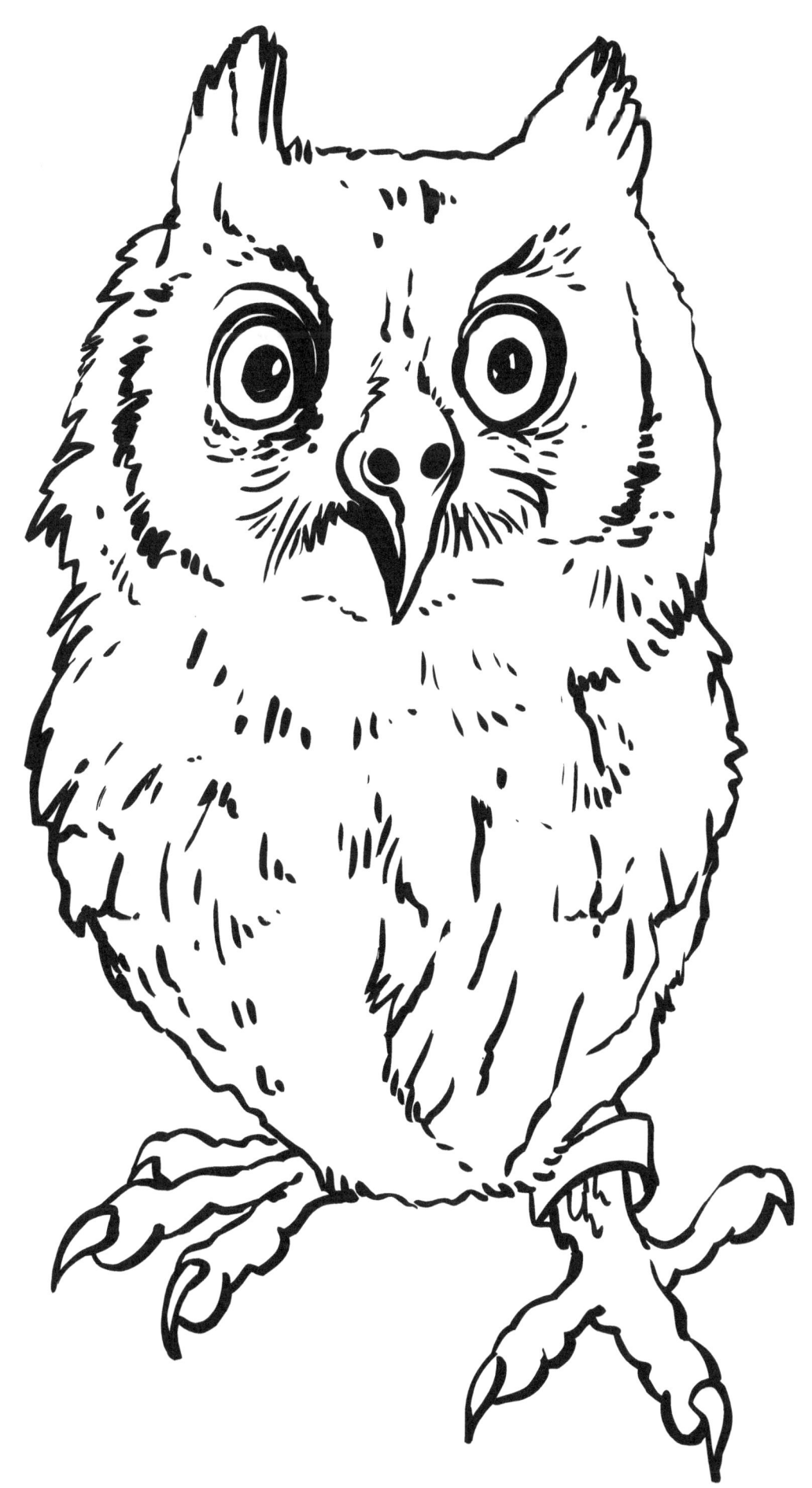

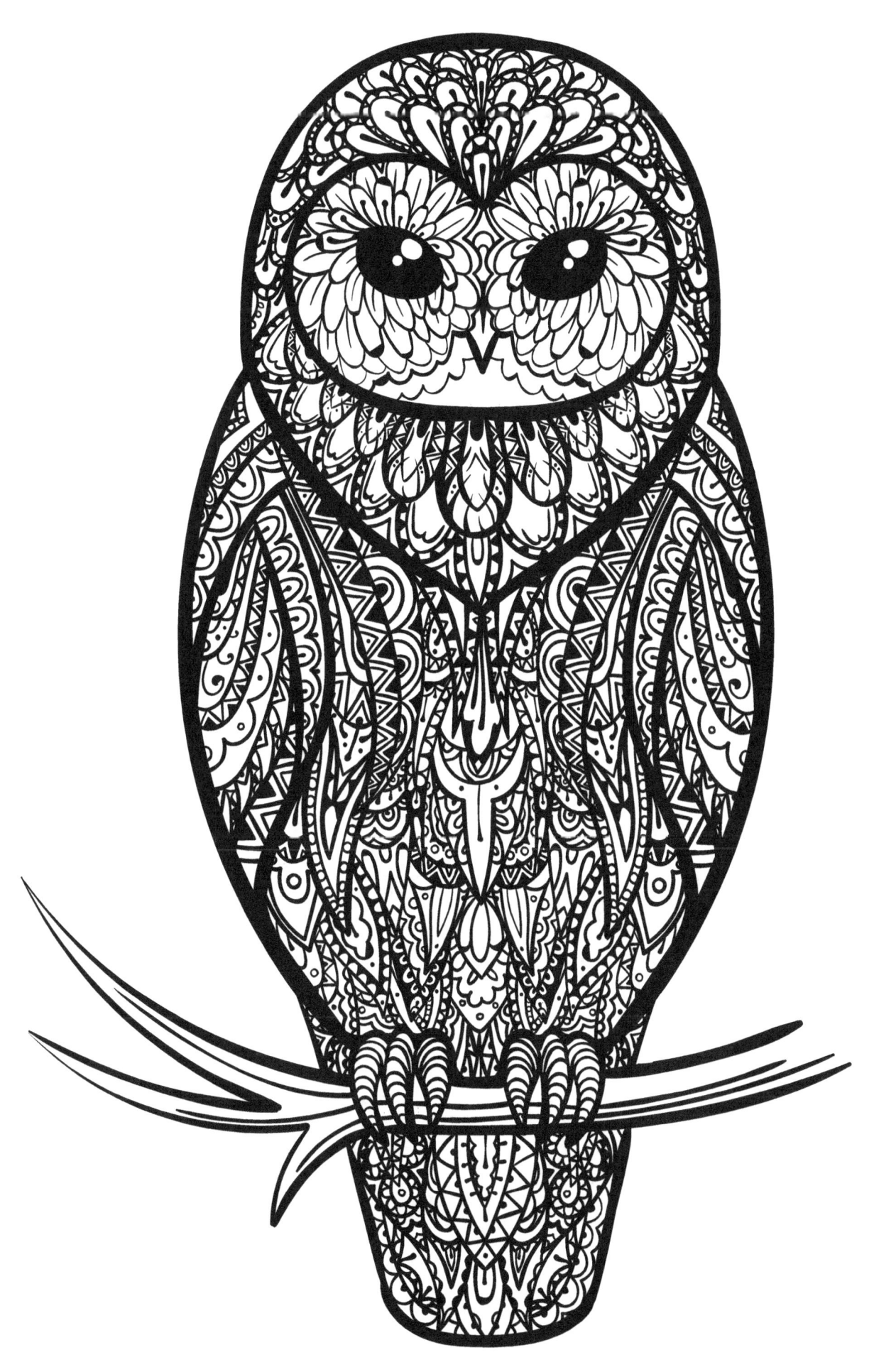

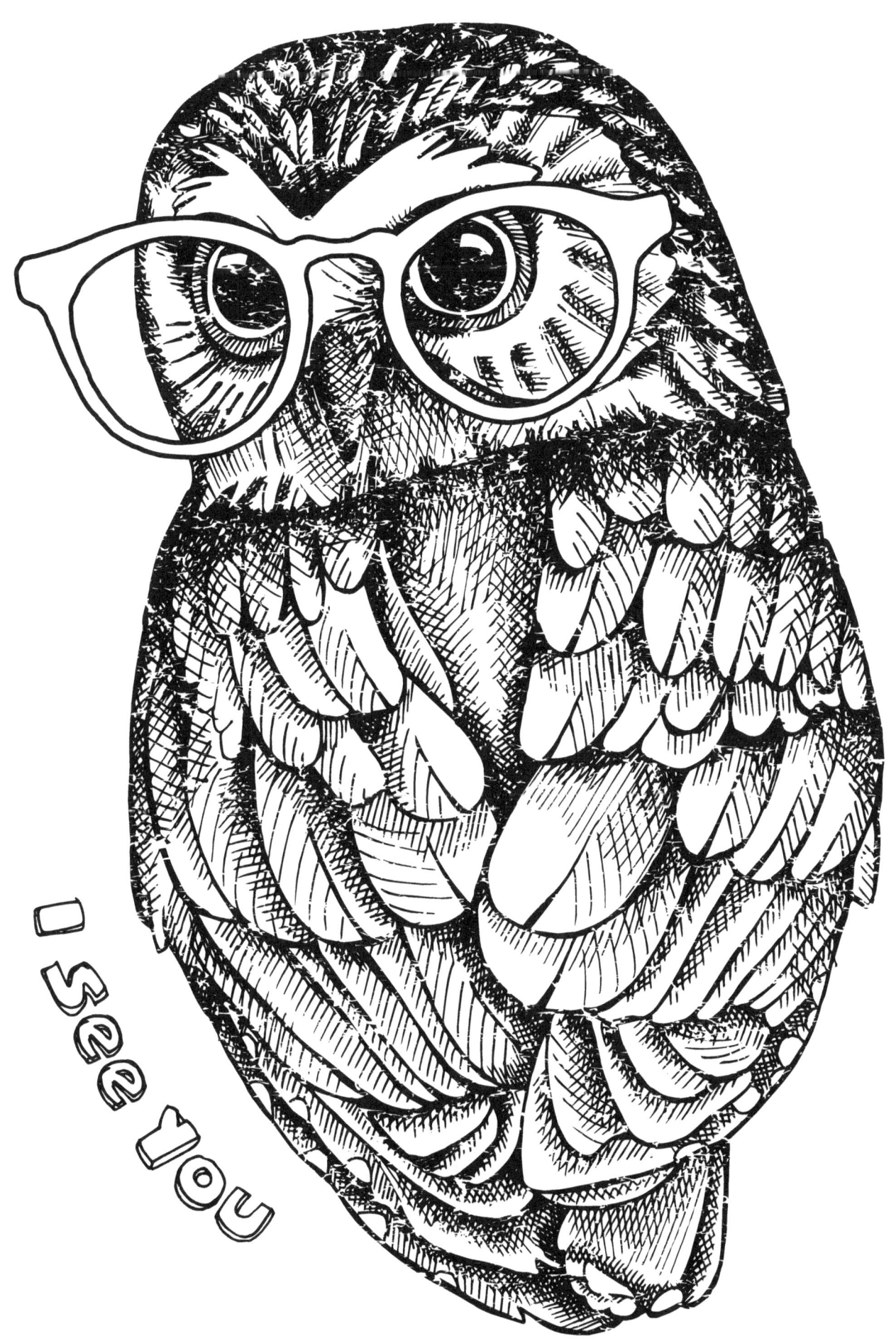

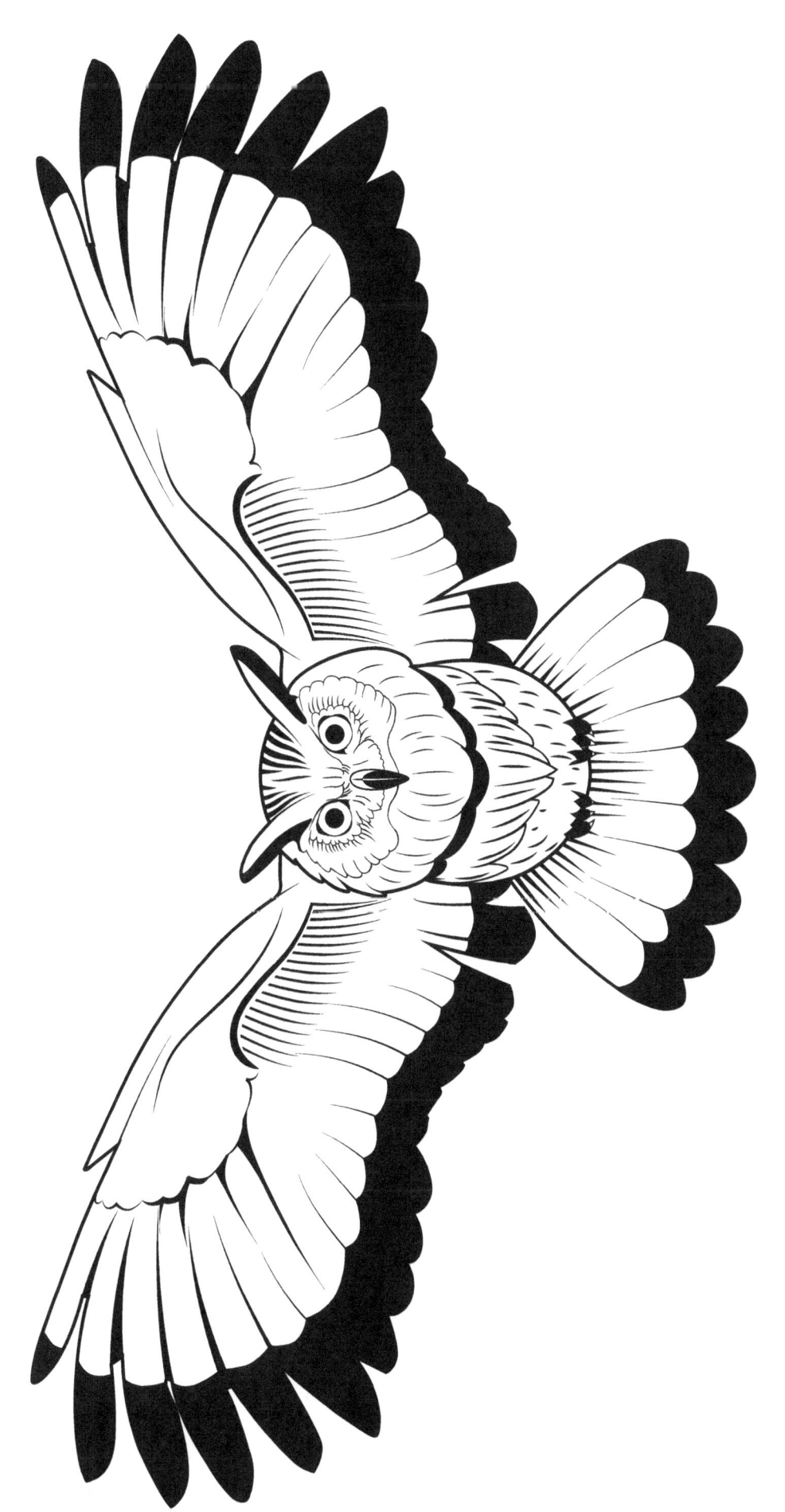